Almost a Catastrophe!
A Welsh Family's Adventures in Malta

Janet Corke

Almost a Catastrophe!
© Janet Corke 2021

Published 2021 by The Artel Press
ISBN 978-1-7399003-0-4

Janet Corke asserts the moral right to be identified as the author of this work.

This memoir is a faithful account of our adventures only insofar as my memory is truthful!

Also by Janet Corke:
A Hidden Home in the Gwydyr Forest

Printed in the UK by Imprint Academic Ltd

For Nic, Charlotte and Emma

'Every time you leave home,
another road takes you into
a world you were never in'
John O'Donohue

Index

page

Prologue   1

Chapter 1   On Our Way   3
Chapter 2   Almost a Catastrophe!   8
Chapter 3   Early Days   13
Chapter 4   Civilians on an Aircraft Carrier   19
Chapter 5   Maltese Medicine   24
Chapter 6   Exploring   31
Chapter 7   House Hunting   40
Chapter 8   Decision Time   46
Chapter 9   Birkirkara   52
Chapter 10   Our New Home   56
Chapter 11   Nain's Visit   65
Chapter 12   Mushrooms   71
Chapter 13   Doris   76
Chapter 14   Our Friend Fred   81
Chapter 15   'Normal Friends'   89
Chapter 16   Party, Party, Party!   94
Chapter 17   Christmas 1963   101
Chapter 18   Independence   110
Chapter 19   Charlotte   118
Chapter 20   Moving On - or Not?   125
Chapter 21   Festa 1965   132
Chapter 22   A Bombshell   136
Chapter 23   The Little House   141
Chapter 24   Going Home   148
Chapter 25   Sailing By   156

Afterword   161

Glossary

Auberge	Grand lodging house for the Knights of St.John
Ajjut!	Help!
Cisk	Beer produced on the Island
Cornette	Type of wimple worn by nuns
Cymanfa Ganu	Singing Festival (Welsh)
Djhaisa	Maltese gondola - water taxi
Faldetta	Woman's head dress and cloak
Fenkata	Rabbit stew, national Maltese dish
Festa	Religious Festival
Gecko	Small lizard
Grandpa	Charlie's father
Grandma	Charlie's mother
Grigalata	Strong north-easterly wind
Iva	Yes
lx-Xorti	Good luck
Karozzin	Horse drawn carriage
L'imnarja	Feast for Farmers after harvest in June
Luzzu	Traditional fishing boat
Nain	Jan's Mother (Welsh)
Pavaljuni	Hand-painted flags
Taid	Jan's father (Welsh)
Sahha	Goodbye

PROLOGUE

Driving from Liverpool to Malta for a holiday in 1971, with three children aged ten, six and two, would not have been everyone's idea of a holiday – but then neither would living in a ruined cottage in Snowdonia have been every young couple's dream home.

The cottage fulfilled Charlie Corke's ambition to live in the mountains of Snowdonia. Brought up in Liverpool during the Second World War, a week each summer on a farm in North Wales was his only escape from the bombed city. As a teenager he survived three years as a conscript in a Lancashire coalmine before qualifying as a civil engineer in his mid twenties. After obtaining a job in the Conwy Valley he spent his spare time searching for a cottage he could afford to buy, and in 1956 found Ty'n yr Ardd. Accessible only on foot, with no drainage or electricity, its only asset was a nearby stream, and scraping together one hundred and ten pounds he became the owner of a semi-derelict cottage.

Meanwhile, in the harbour town of Conwy (apart from three intervals of six months at Law School in London) I was toiling my way through five years of training to become a solicitor. Born and brought up in Llanrwst in the Conwy Valley life had little by way of entertainment in 1956 apart from an amateur dramatic society which I had joined. Great excitement had ensued when three, unmarried, young men arrived and also joined the society. All civil engineers working on hydroelectricity schemes in the mountains, they included a rather mysterious man who lived in a remote cottage in the Gwydyr Forest, above Llanrwst.

The story of our lives in the cottage is told elsewhere. It ended abruptly in July 1963 when Charlie announced his next job was in Malta. Four weeks later we flew to the tiny Island in the Mediterranean, midway between Europe and Africa, to spend three years on 'Melita, the Land of Honey'. For those wishing to expand their knowledge of Malta, Gozo and Comino please seek out the many books written by eminent historians and archaeologists, architects and geologists. This book is the story of a family's life sixty years ago, living as civilians on what Sir Winston Churchill described as "an unsinkable aircraft carrier."

Malta in the nineteen sixties - heat, dust, torrential rain, siesta, church bells, fireworks, shoats, potholed roads, red letter boxes, shoeless children, village women knitting, glamorous city women, small nuns under large wimples, unreliable electricity, salty drinking water, octopus stew, England winning the World Football Cup the day we left – all memories of life on the Island.

ON OUR WAY!

"You're going to live in Malta? Our wartime prime minister described the Island as an unsinkable aircraft carrier!" Raising her eyebrows almost up to her hairline, my great-aunt continued "seventeen miles long and nine miles wide! It's just a brown, lump of rock in the middle of the sea! You'll be bored stiff!" She never missed an opportunity to remind me that "I have travelled to many exotic places my dear," and such was her verdict when I told her that Charlie's work was taking us to live abroad for two years.

"Well, I have read a bit about it – did you know it was called 'Melita' by the Romans, because of the honey?" I asked.

"Honey? Never! Nothing grows there" she pronounced.

My mother was equally dismissive when I gave her the news. "Will you be able to work there?" she asked.

I had been waiting for this challenge and grimaced. "Unfortunately, I won't" I replied.

"Why ever not? It's still a colony isn't it, so why won't our law apply? How civilised is it there? I know they had a terrible time during the War, but till then no-one had ever heard of Malta."

"It has a very long history and their legal system goes back for centuries, and Britain has never done anything to change it" was my rather lame response.

"Is that so?" she replied sardonically. Realising she had been somewhat harsh she continued "Oh Jan, you've only been qualified for three years, you've bought your car, and now you'll have to leave it behind!"

"Well, Charlie says we can have it exported to Malta as part of our contract so it's coming with us."

Perhaps she had good reason to complain. I had qualified as a solicitor in 1960 and spent my first six months' salary on a second hand convertible Morris Minor. Shortly afterwards I married Charlie who had been working on a hydro-electric scheme in Blaenau Ffestiniog in North Wales. Due to be opened by the Queen in August 1963 we had assumed he would then be appointed to a new project in the UK, and going abroad to work came as a complete surprise.

He had bought his cottage in Snowdonia before I knew him, and the restoration work was far from complete. The arrival of Nic, now a typical two year old, had allowed me little time to practise my chosen profession, and I had been job hunting when news came of our imminent departure to Malta. With packing to organise and our departure date a mere four weeks away, knowledge of the legal system in our future home was hardly my priority.

We left Heathrow on the 15th August 1963, a cold wet morning, and stepped onto the runway in Naples into a seemingly impenetrable wall of heat. After re-fuelling we continued to Malta arriving at Luqa airport late in the afternoon and I was distinctly unimpressed by the sight of a few shabby sheds and three strips of glistening tarmac. With the temperature at almost a hundred degrees we carried our hand luggage and raincoats into what looked like an old RAF hanger.

With no luggage carousel we, and the other passengers, were instructed to wait until our suitcases were brought from the plane. "I'd have thought the airport would be bigger and more modern than this - the War ended eighteen years ago. Surely someone should have sorted the place out before now!" I exclaimed.

Rather exasperated Charlie replied "I know, but there are some photographs on the wall over there showing the wartime damage. Go and have a look, and I'll hang on to Nic."

A photograph of a plane with the caption 'Ala Littoria 1926' had a note explaining how the Italian Airline had requested a refuelling stop on Malta during its scheduled flights from Libya to Italy, concluding 'passengers are aware of the lack of tarmacadam runways' – presumably warning them to hang on tight to their seats when landing.

One of the larger photographs was of three biplanes called Faith, Hope and Charity which, the caption told me, had provided the grand total of Malta's aerial defence capability on the 11th June 1940, the day a bombing campaign by the Italians had started and, with no opposition, had continued for several days. However, by December 1940 the Island's civilian airport had been transformed into an RAF Station with machine gun posts, a bomb dump, hangers, barracks and all the personnel required to operate as a base for Hurricanes and Wellington Bombers.

Just as I was looking at a large black and white photograph of the airport showing bomb craters in the rough ground and a partially demolished building, Charlie called "Jan, our stuff's arrived." A notice underneath explained how, at the end of the War, despite having been severely damaged, Luqa continued with its dual role as Malta's civilian air terminal for the newly set up Air Malta Ltd., as well as the RAF Officers' Mess. The present passenger terminal, financed by Britain, had opened in 1958 and provided a small cafe, a Post Office, a Cable and Wireless office, toilets and a viewing balcony – this is where we had landed.

A team of stocky men ran back and forth, shouting out the names on the labels until passengers claimed their luggage. Officious looking, but polite, men in smart police uniforms, each with a gun in a holster around his waist, led us to a counter, where it took three inspections of our documents before our passports were stamped and they waved us on our way.

Out in the blistering sunshine we spotted an ancient Hillman Minx sporting a 'taxi' sign on its front number plate, and sank into the rear seats as the driver loaded our suitcases into the boot, our only possessions until our tea chests and the car arrived – hopefully in the not too distant future.

We set off at a furious speed along rough, bumpy roads, in and out of potholes, the driver hooting and waving his arms for no obvious reason. Slow processions, accompanied by loud brass bands, filled the narrow streets of several villages as we drove past in the late afternoon light until, in one of the larger villages, we were forced to a halt.

An elderly lady dressed in black was standing at the side of the road, by a bus stop. She was wearing a faldetta, a stiff, crescent-shape black hood in the form of a combined headdress and shawl. Covering her head but not her face, it fell down to her calves as she clasped the side of the faldetta with her right hand so that the material was draped to one side, like a sail. Nic stared at her, whilst I wondered if she would be able to get on a bus.

"She will be much cooler than we are!" Charlie exclaimed. "The sail catches any breeze inside the hood and women on the islands have worn them for centuries!"

A huge statue of the Madonna, rocking dangerously on a plinth decorated with plastic flowers, processed slowly past, a team of men under the heavy wooden structure straining to hold their precious burden upright, sweat running down their faces. We all sat in silence until Nic suddenly shouted "Look, look a lady up there!"

The mysterious and alluring faldetta.

The taxi driver turned to us and, smiling broadly, said "Many, many festas in Malta. Today is one of our big days, the Feast of the Assumption, as you will know."

Apologetically we, as non-Catholics, could only nod and smile back.

After about twenty minutes the procession disappeared down a narrow street and we restarted our journey, the driver furiously revving his engine as we careered into our first experience of Maltese fireworks. A sudden almighty boom crashed around us, followed by several more in quick succession, and before we had recovered the sky was multi-coloured, awash with light from innumerable fireworks, red, blue, green, as we hurtled along the dusty roads in a daze of amazement and apprehension.

ALMOST A CATASTROPHE!

For Malta and Gozo to succeed as tourist destinations, and to establish commercial enterprises on the islands, it was essential to increase both the electricity supply and the availability of fresh water. We were soon to discover that the electricity supply had historically been erratic, and even in larger towns such as Mosta and Birkirkara many families still had no electrical appliances, using paraffin cookers and fridges. In the villages, as darkness approached, ladies sitting on hard chairs by their front door, usually knitting furiously, and old men smoking and watching the world go by, went inside, shut their wooden doors, closed their shutters and went to bed.

The only reliable source of water was the sea and, to collect and store fresh water, houses were built with flat roofs which caught the rain which was directed down through internal pipes into cisterns below ground. Over the ages this system had provided sufficient water throughout the summer months whilst waiting for September storms and heavy winter showers to refill the underground reservoirs and galleries, but now modern times required modern methods. Charlie had been appointed as the deputy resident engineer for the construction of an innovative power station cum seawater desalination plant, due to be completed in two years but, in the end, took three.

His firm had booked us into a hotel in Sliema. At last the taxi screeched to a halt outside a large, three storey, limestone block building, with tall narrow windows each with a balcony

8

overlooking the sea. The driver cheerfully carried our luggage up the steps to a huge wooden door which opened into a spacious, cool reception area. We had been told that the Maltese language was a mixture of Arabic and Italian, but many people also spoke English particularly in the areas frequented by tourists such as Valetta and Sliema. To our relief a small man sitting behind a high counter called out "Mr. and Mrs. Corke we welcome you to our new, modern hotel" and rushed forward to shake our hands and pat Nic on the head.

All was clean and welcoming, with beautiful multi-coloured tiled floors and a semi-sophisticated bar with gleaming bottles of every drink I had ever heard of ranged behind it. The lounge overlooked the promenade and was furnished with brightly coloured, unyielding easy chairs, whilst the sparkling sea beyond disappeared into the distance. After much handshaking and warm smiles and after scooping Nic up and whirling him round, the owner said he would escort us our room.

"Of course, of course, we have many en-suite rooms in our new hotel and this is the quiet season so, Mr. and Mrs. Corke, we have reserved the best room for you, with a sea view of course! Come, come!" and he disappeared, with Nic perched on his shoulders.

A very new lift took us up to the first floor where the corridor was littered with ladders, tools, plasterboard, lengths of wood and pots of paint. Our room was large and overlooked the sea, with high ceilings from which hung a very modern electric fan whirring noisily as it stirred the hot air to no cooling effect whatsoever. A big bed with an ornate, highly polished wooden frame, sat at one end with a small bed for Nic nearby. Mosquito nets hung over the beds and a curtain made of coloured plastic strips flapped noisily against the open window. It appeared comfortable enough, and having decided we would have a rest before finding somewhere to eat Charlie went downstairs to enquire about possible restaurants.

I discovered that our 'en suite' meant it had a functioning loo and a large washbasin but no shower or bath. Having been returned by the hotel manager with much laughter and hand clapping Nic was still firing on all cylinders. He had had a nap on the plane and I decided to stand him in the basin to cool him down. The taps worked and the basin filled with water, and after washing him I reached out to pick up a towel from a nearby chair and turned back to Nic. As I put my hands on him to lift him out an electric shock shot through my body.

I stood, petrified, unable to move, my eyes desperately searching for an explanation. I did not have far to look. Out of the wall above Nic's head protruded an electric wire, obviously intended for a wall lamp, with bare ends sticking out of the cloth fabric insulation and, curious as usual, he had reached out and grasped it.

Again I tried to lift him out but his finger was stuck to the wire. Aghast, I ran into the corridor screaming "Charlie, Charlie where are you? Nic has been electrocuted!"

Workmen suddenly appeared waving their arms, running from room to room, yelling in Maltese at one another as Charlie stepped out of the lift into chaos. Calm and collected as usual he picked up a small length of wood from the floor, ran into our room and as I shouted "No, no it's not Nic's fault !" he brought the wood down sharply on the wire which immediately broke, leaving Nic standing in the water with his small hand in the air, staring at everyone.

With tears running down my face I grabbed him, and as I was trying to wrap a towel round his slippery body a man in a suit appeared, accompanied by the owner shouting and wringing his hands. They pushed their way through the workmen crowded around the doorway both obviously totally bewildered at the sight of a man holding a length of wood, a woman crying, holding a toddler who was soaking wet all talking at once.

"Who is this?" I cried. "We need an ambulance!"

"Madam, please, please, I am a doctor. Let me see you and the child."

"Where did you come from? How do I know you're a doctor?" I sobbed.

"Madam, I was having a Cisk in the lounge and heard much commotion and came to help an unfortunate person, if required."

This was my first experience of the careful, formal manner of speech employed by educated Maltese when speaking English, as he continued "You and your child are both alive. Please explain to me the circumstances of this unhappy situation."

As I gabbled incoherently he carefully examined Nic, and then me before sitting back. "How very fortunate that the child was wet all over his body so that the electric current went around him but you, Mrs. Corke, were very fortunate also that our electricity supply is not very efficient, but I advise a visit to our excellent hospital to make sure all is well."

He took us to the hospital in his own old, but very luxurious car, ushering us in to a large, cool building where we were immediately surrounded by nuns, each wearing a long white habit and an enormous wimple, which I learned later was called a 'cornette'. Until then apparently unfazed by events, Nic took fright at these kindly but strange figures and howled miserably whilst another doctor carefully examined us both until he was satisfied that, apart from a small burn mark on his finger, Nic was none the worse, and neither was I. Taking us back to the hotel our doctor congratulated us again on our lucky escape and, assuring us of his attention at all times, pressed his card into my hand and drove away.

Back at the hotel we were objects of great curiosity to the

other guests as well as the staff, and were plied with food and drink to the point of embarrassment. Eventually we escaped to our room and Nic, at last tired, was prepared to go to sleep. I gazed at our big bed desperate to close my eyes so that I would not see the washbasin, but could imagine myself in our cool Welsh cottage, away from the heat and the noise drifting in from the promenade below.

Suddenly Charlie said "I must go out now to meet Paul – sorry I forgot to tell you."

I stared at him. Was there to be no end to this bizarre day? "Who is Paul?" I asked as I lay on the bed.

"He's the resident engineer, you know, in charge of the whole job" he explained.

Exhausted I simply replied "Fine. Just don't wake me when you get back" and closed my eyes, leaving him to rummage in our big suitcase for a clean shirt. After he left I stared at the whirring fan hoping it might hypnotise me to sleep, then put my fingers in my ears trying to blot out the incessant chatter audible from below despite the closed shutters, but nothing worked - oblivion escaped me.

When I knew Nic was fast asleep I changed and wandered down to the lounge where other guests, mostly Italian, nodded and smiled at me but I retreated to a corner and asked a waiter for a glass of water. Shaking his head he said "Madam, please I do not think water is good for you. It is better you have a Cisk." I nodded, having no idea what a Cisk was, but when it arrived it was pleasant and very cold, and I downed it in one go without a glance at the label.

Two hours later I tried to appear calm and collected when Charlie and Paul returned, and everything was fine - except that they found me, somewhat inebriated, with six empty bottles of the local 'Cisk' beer scattered about the table in front of me.

EARLY DAYS

Despite effusive apologies from the hotel management I was desperate to leave. The local 'mafia' went into overdrive, and within two days Paul had found a small house up a dusty lane near Sliema.

Only a few doors away from his own flat it meant Charlie could have a lift to the construction site every day with him and, although my heart sank when I saw the tiny yard at the back, we took the house for three months at the princely sum of fifteen pounds per month. We repacked our suitcases, shook hands with the staff, thanked them for their help, piled everything into a taxi and left the hotel, vowing never to return.

The house had recently been built in the garden of a large house next door. Owned by two elderly sisters, they were very polite but somewhat forbidding in manner. The younger lady would occasionally smile and nod if she saw me, but her sister maintained a frosty distance.

In the living room two old-fashioned easy chairs and a matching sofa, all overstuffed and very uncomfortable, were lined up along one wall, whilst a wooden drop-leaf table covered with a floral plastic cloth and three hard upright chairs sat next to the only window, which looked out onto the lane. Off the living room a dark, narrow kitchen was equipped with a two ring electric cooker, a very small fridge, a frying pan and a couple of saucepans, a kettle, a few knives, forks and spoons, plastic tumblers and some hideous, thick crockery. Despite two colourful pictures of the sea, and a vase of artificial flowers on the table, the whole ground floor gave an impression of deep gloom.

Upstairs the larger bedroom had a small, metal double bed with a horse hair mattress, two very lumpy pillows, all overhung by a huge mosquito net, a chest of drawers and a single size wardrobe. The second bedroom had a single bed with a modern mattress and one pillow, a smaller mosquito net and a chair. Fortunately bedding was provided and would be changed twice a week. In the bathroom the loo only flushed after the water tank on the roof had refilled - very slowly - and it took half an hour to cover the bottom of the big old fashioned bath with an inch of water.

A door in the small bedroom opened onto a staircase leading to the flat roof where ropes were stretched from side to side for hanging out the washing. There we could sit in the evening and take in our spectacular view across countless flat rooftops, each with its assortment of multi coloured washing flapping and dancing in the wind, way over as far as Grand Harbour full of ships - but not until we had plastered insect repellent on every inch of bare skin to ward off the large, vicious mosquitos.

Our belongings, including my Morris Minor, were somewhere on the high seas, so in the meantime we would have to "make do" (no change there) and try to settle into this almost empty, impersonal little house "in the middle of bedlam" as Charlie grumbled. All around wirelesses blared, motor horns beeped, dogs barked, children cried, bells rang and fireworks banged "to frighten off the devil" as he claimed. Two days later, in self-defence, he bought a transistor radio, still a relatively modern wonder in the 1960s.

After our first very hot, uncomfortable night Charlie

went to work with Paul and I decided to do some shopping and, with the temperature just short of a hundred degrees, I strapped Nic into his pushchair and set off to catch the bus to Sliema. The younger sister had told me that the larger shops had fridges storing frozen meat (although it was imported from Australia and only arrived every three months), as well as fish. Fresh vegetables were sometimes available, and they stocked pasteurised milk.

An old grey donkey

On the main road at the bottom of the lane pre-war models of Fords, Hillmans, Morris and Austin cars raced past on a tarmac surface shimmering with the heat. As I watched the constant stream of traffic it dawned on me that, without a car, frozen meat or fish would have melted before I was even half way home, and milk was a non-starter. Abandoning the idea I returned to the house – until my car arrived our diet would be limited by what came in tins, the local flat bread which was rock hard by the following day and tomatoes, potatoes, cabbage and pomegranates, all of which I could buy from a man who pushed his hand cart round the nearby streets and alleys. The water was safe to drink, but always tasted salty, and with no bottled water we drank either black coffee or the local beer with fizzy lemonade for Nic - which made him even more active than usual.

A large banana tree grew in the back yard providing welcome shade and a small space for Nic to play, and the lane did have one diversion - the donkey. The lane was a dead end, where a dilapidated wooden hut was home for an old, grey donkey whose owner was also old, with a wizened face and two teeth permanently clamped around a cigarette. Twice every day, always at the same time, he came to fetch the donkey and led it away, returning two hours later. Nic was fascinated by the ungainly, unlovely animal and we had to stand outside the house to watch as it plodded past, stirring up the dust, braying loudly, its huge eyes swivelling, the owner stopping to pat Nic on the head as they went by. One morning sheet lightning, rolling thunder and torrential rain made a welcome change to the endless sunshine, and an hour of a tropical-style downpour turned our roof into a mini swimming pool as Nic danced around clapping his hands, shouting "beach, beach" – and missed his treat of watching the donkey go past.

I was very curious to see where Charlie would be working, and on the first Sunday we investigated the bus system. We knew that all buses started and finished their journeys at the bus terminal in Floriana outside Valetta. "The building site is on the side of Marsa Creek" Charlie said, "so we'll have to change buses twice . The foreman told me that Floriana is in the middle of the Island, and roads to everywhere fan out from there."

The first bus took us to Floriana. We alighted on to a huge flat area, with low, ancient buildings on two sides, and could see the massive Kingsgate leading into Valetta at the far end. "He told me there are granaries under here" Charlie continued as we waited for our next bus. "They could never grow wheat here and got supplies from Sicily, so these large under-ground stores were built in the seventeenth century by the Knights, and they only stopped using them last year."

The sun was beating down, and with no sign of our next bus I asked plaintively "Shall we go home?"

Buses were few and far between, but eventually we arrived at the construction site. Finding a use for the redundant dockyards was an integral part of the UK's strategy to modernise and industrialise Malta, and the empty land on the Marsa Creek was the obvious place to build the new power station. A large area of semi derelict land, with enormous, empty sheds and bits of broken machinery scattered around the edges, was my first view of the site. With the sun reflecting off the white limestone it was baking hot and the heat was barely tolerable. The following day, to his dismay, Charlie learnt that whilst the rest of the Island slumbered between the hours of twelve and three, at the construction site his working hours were the usual British routine of eight until five, heat or no heat.

We rose at six in the morning whilst it was still cool, and Charlie went off to work at seven. Nic slept for two hours after lunch and then refused to sleep until it was time for us all to go to bed at nine. Heat and dust governed what you wore and where and when you went out, but week by week the temperature gradually cooled to the mid-eighties in the shade, and soon the Maltese workmen told Charlie that, for them, swimming was over because it was too cold. We were still too hot, our skin tacky and wet, and although I hated crawling under the mosquito net, a painful mosquito bite on my leg after sitting on the roof one evening quickly persuaded me that the stifling heat inside the net was a price worth paying.

The change from clean mountain air at the cottage to the humidity and dust on the Island was dramatic, and within days Nic had a cough. Night after night the more he coughed the hotter he got and the hotter he got the more he coughed. Realisation dawned - there was no national health system in Malta! In desperation Charlie suggested we gave him rum in warm water. "We can't do that!" I exclaimed, my Welsh non-conformist upbringing coming to the fore.

"It won't hurt him if we try it" he replied. "I remember being given it when I was a kid and I had a bad cough." I was very doubtful but that evening he came home with a small bottle of rum.

I said primly "Nic will probably hate it" - Nic loved it!

"More, more!" he yelled excitedly, and we had no more sleepless nights, with the bottle on the top of the wardrobe, well out of reach.

After about three weeks a long letter arrived from Grandpa all about the work he had been doing at the cottage, which sent Charlie into a decline. Muttering under his breath I heard "I wish I could spirit myself back there for a few days! Oh, for one of those cool, clear autumn evenings at the cottage!" To console himself he settled in one of the very uncomfortable chairs to listen to a symphony on the World Service where Nic found him, climbed on his knee, then fell asleep in his lap, and where I found them both when I returned from gathering the washing from the roof.

CIVILIANS ON AN AIRCRAFT-CARRIER

Ever since the Knights of St. John had arrived on Malta in 1530 and moored their fleet of galleys and three-masted carracks in Grand Harbour the Island had been a naval base. After Lord Nelson's invasion in 1800 the islands became part of Queen Victoria's empire and, following their usual custom, the English established an administrative system to rule over the islanders. After the Second World War change was inevitable. Gradually, the number of civilian administrators dwindled away, leaving behind the Services personnel who had little, if any, day to day contact with the Maltese people other than as employer and employee in the dockyards, or as domestic servants. It took me some time to understand the way things worked.

Desperate to get Nic out of the house I had spotted a children's playground nearby and set off in the late afternoons as the weather cooled, looking hopefully for other British children as playmates. Never having previously experienced a playground Nic immediately loved the high slide, the swings and the roundabout, and within a few minutes a swarm of local children would descend on us, take over and keep him entertained for at least an hour, but there were no other English parents there and, as I watched, I wondered why children whose parents were in the Services did not come out to play.

Shortly after we arrived the local way of doing things became clearer. One late afternoon we caught a bus to the promenade at Sliema, and searched for a sandy patch amongst the rocks so that Nic could have a paddle and settled down on a small area of the fine limestone grit. He stood still, slowly put one foot forward, ran back, then in again, before sitting down and clapping his hands as small waves washed over him.

At intervals along the beach pits about four or five feet deep had been cut into the soft limestone, then extended by digging channels about two feet wide into the sea at either end so that the water was always changing. Two large Maltese families arrived, smiling at us as they walked past, and stopped near one of the pits. Out of a large basket came a picnic of bread and tomato paste, whilst two babies crawled in the sand and older children ran in and out of the sea, always careful to avoid splashing two elderly ladies who had been gently lowered onto fold up chairs.

Immediately the children spotted us, and within minutes Nic had disappeared amongst them as they shouted to him to join them in the water. After a while Charlie said "I'd better check he's alright," and wandering over stood on the edge of one of the pits talking to one of the mothers. Running up behind him, Nic caught him off guard, gave him a push - and in Charlie went, displacing most of the water and soaking the young mother. There was a moment of startled embarrassment - until the other mother and the grandmothers all slapped their hands over their mouths, whilst the fathers nudged one another grinning broadly before everyone started to clap and laugh.

Apologising, and at the same time feeling both foolish and embarrassed, Charlie decided he had better join in and shouted to Nic "Come on, jump in!" - which he did, down to the bottom of the pit.

Fishing him out, spluttering and coughing, Charlie said sternly "You must come back with us now" but the young mother, still laughing, replied "Come, come, he can be with us. It is no problem," and Nic immediately re-joined the family. As

Charlie walked back I looked all around the beach, then realised we were the only British people there, so presumed Nic was a welcome novelty.

On our next trip the sea was unusually rough, but Nic ran straight in until the water was up to his chest, washing him off his feet. He managed to keep his head above water until Charlie got to him and pulled him out, and within days he was swimming as well as the local boys. Again there were no other British families on the beach and I asked Charlie "I wonder why we never see any other Britishers here?"

Our third weekend loomed and, still with no car, "Oh, for a wet day and some trees!" I grumbled, the heat bearing down on me in our stuffy little house.

"I know" Charlie replied, "but the foreman told me there are trees in Buskett Gardens. Come on, let's go now! We'll have to find a bus that goes to Siggiewi." We rattled along objects of some surprise to the other travellers and, about an hour later hot and dishevelled, we arrived in a mini forest. Many of the trees were native conifers, whilst others were familiar deciduous varieties, and, much to our surprise, several trees had fruit on them. Again, although we were the only British family to be seen, a couple of hours in the shade amongst groups of friendly local people, walking or picnicking, made the uncomfortable journey so worthwhile that we decided we would visit Buskett again, particularly when we learnt that, centuries ago, the Island had been covered with trees - until they had all been cut down to build ships, just as happened to the forests in Snowdonia.

When we (eventually) had the car again, we found the long, sandy beach at Mellieha near St. Paul's Bay where, according to the Acts of the Apostles, a ship taking Saint Paul and other prisoners to Rome in 60AD ran into a great storm and sought shelter on the Island. The local people went to the beaches at the weekends, and hordes of young boys would whisk Nic off to play, and with his black hair and tanned skin he became indistinguishable from the local children. Disappearing into their midst, he would re-appear with a chunk of bread spread with tomato paste, stay for a few minutes and then dash off again. We settled down one afternoon for an interval of peace, knowing Nic was safe in the midst of a crowd of young boys watching a game of football.

"Have you noticed there are no seagulls dive-bombing for bits of food here?" I murmured lazily. "I wonder why?" Happily comatose, an imaginary, gentle, warm drizzle on my face rather than the hot, dry breeze blowing off the sea, lost in the tall, whispering pine trees of the Gwydyr Forest, my dream was suddenly shattered.

Shouting "come, come!" a large group of older lads came running towards us, a blood spattered Nic held aloft by three of them, the others waving their arms and yelling at one another. They handed Nic, now screaming as loudly as everyone else, to Charlie who set him down on the sand where we could immediately see he had no broken bones.

"The ball, the ball, he hit me, he hit me!" sobbed Nic.

His only injury was a nose bleed from a soft beach ball landing on his head. I wiped the blood off his face and hands as the lads, obviously very relieved, returned to their game, only to be re-joined by Nic five minutes later when they shouted "Alright? Come, come!"

As he ran back towards the other youngsters his fond father said, with a sigh, "Ah well, where there's no sense there's no reason," and settled back to his book.

Before drifting into another doze I said "the beach is really crowded but we are the only British family. It's so odd, I can't understand it."

He laughed. "Jan, we've nowhere else to go! Didn't you realise the Service families never use the beaches because they go to their Club!"

Nic with new friends

MALTESE MEDICINE

A month or so after we arrived Charlie came home with good news. The ship carrying our car and our belongings had arrived, and he could collect them from the docks the following afternoon. Nic and I waited by the gate until, at last, I heard the familiar sound of my Morris Minor chugging up the lane from the main road.

"Why is Charlie going so slowly?" asked Nic.

"That's why!" I replied. The hood was down and our tea chests were piled up all around him. "My poor old car! Where are we going to put all our things?" There was nowhere to put our belongings, and the tea chests remained unpacked, stacked up in the yard as a constant reminder that we needed to find a bigger house.

Towards the end of September Charlie developed spots on his face. Having the National Health Service at home we were at a loss until I remembered the doctor who had come to the hotel on our first day. We had never received a bill from him, but as we were living in a British colony we naively assumed health care was free. His surgery was in Sliema and I persuaded Charlie to make an appointment for the next day. "Ah, Mr. Corke, and how is your dear wife and the little child? I trust they are well after the most unfortunate incident on the day of your arrival on our Island."

The formal manner of speech was always a surprise, but

Charlie hid a smile as he replied "Thank you, Doctor, they are well but as you can see I now have a problem." The doctor immediately diagnosed the spots as impetigo, said he had probably contracted it on the building site, and sent him home with strict instructions about hygiene, a small tube of antibiotic cream – and a large bill. By the next day Nic and I also had spots which cleared quickly with the antibiotic cream, but not Charlie. Every time he shaved the infection spread and I became more concerned as new spots appeared whilst he, usually never depressed or anxious, was obviously very miserable.

"I feel like a leper!" he exclaimed one evening, "and I should go about with a little bell and call out unclean, unclean."

"Don't you think you're being a bit dramatic?" I asked unkindly, but the next day we agreed he should see a skin specialist. He decided to talk to the foreman on the site who, we reasoned, would have local knowledge of how best to deal with the problem. A kindly, middle aged man with a large family and much respected by the local workforce, he gave Charlie an address in Valetta.

"There is a specialist professor in Valetta, very well known, very good" he told him. "You go to that address - and he will always see you" he added, rather mysteriously.

After the Great Siege the Knights built Valetta on the Sciberras Peninsula, a narrow strip of land separating Grand Harbour from Marsamxett Harbour. After strengthening the original fortifications they continued the expansion of the new city further and further up the hill from the sea. Soon palaces, magnificent churches and grand inns, known as auberges, were built in Republic Street, the city's spine, with streets of houses and small shops branching out on either side leading down-hill to one of the two harbours.

Charlie drove down Republic Street almost to the end of the peninsula, steep streets on either side becoming ever darker, narrowing into cobbled alleyways down to the water. Empty, crumbling buildings stood between old, run-down three storey houses overhanging the roadway shutting out the light, still homes to men in ragged trousers, women in worn thin dresses and shoeless children in shabby clothes, sometimes too large, sometimes too small, who stared as he went past. He turned left into Archbishop Street and inspected the directions on a grubby piece of paper. He read "A very narrow street. The car will not go down it. Triq id-Dejqa."

As he got out of the car children scattered in all directions, leaving a woman standing on the side of the road. Tentatively Charlie approached her holding out his piece of paper which she took, then disappeared inside one of the houses, shouting loudly as she went. Half expecting to be set upon by a horde of children Charlie waited until an elderly man appeared who, smiling broadly, took his arm and led him round a corner to an alley so narrow that poles were stretched across it from balcony to balcony, all laden with washing. Slapping Charlie on the back and pointing down towards the harbour he exclaimed "Good, good, bye, bye" and disappeared into a dark doorway.

Charlie set off on foot and eventually found a rundown building with a shabby brown door, where an almost illegible name-plate confirmed he had come to the right place. With no bell or door knocker he pushed the door which swung open onto a gloomy, empty corridor. He heard voices coming from a nearby room but seeing no-one he went in and, standing in what he assumed was the waiting room, heard a loud conversation in Maltese coming from an adjoining room. The louder and more authoritative voice suddenly swung into English as he heard the Professor telling his unfortunate patient "so if that's what happens put some maggots on it!" Somewhat perturbed Charlie was about to turn round to make a quick exit, but he was too late - the specialist emerged from his consulting room with a young man in a sailor's uniform who scuttled out, his head down.

The Professor beamed at him. "Come in, come in young man." There was no escape. He followed him into a large room with high ceilings and large windows, various medical devices scattered haphazardly over several tables. "Come, come to the window please so I can have a good look at your face – but now I can see there's no need for your concern. It is impetigo - never killed anyone! I make a small charge for your consultation and these remedies - just two good English pounds if you please."

Muttering to himself the Professor opened a cupboard and after moving several bottles around, he handed to Charlie a very large bottle containing a violent purple liquid and a small packet. "Now young man, this medication is to be applied every thirty minutes, and one of these four large tablets is to be taken every six hours for twenty four hours. By this time tomorrow you will see my treatment will have worked a miracle!"

In total disbelief Charlie handed over two pounds and, to be polite, asked when he should go back. The Professor threw his head back and roared with laughter. "My boy, it will not be necessary, but if your affliction has not gone in a week please return and I will dynamite it!" and, patting Charlie on the back, called "Next one please. Goodbye, goodbye."

The liquid regime required Charlie to stay at home but next day there were no new spots, and by the third day he was so much improved that he returned to work. One of the civil engineers was Maltese.

"Ah Charles, it is good you are back, but where have you been?"

"I've got impetigo and found the address of some Professor down by Grand Harbour, but the stuff he gave me does seem to have worked" replied Charlie.

His companion stared at him before starting to laugh then, looking very embarrassed, said "Ah, Charles, did you not know? He sent you down to Strait Street, you know, to the Gut!"

"I didn't know then, but I know now!" Charlie replied with a grin.

"Yes. Some say it's the most famous street in Malta!" his companion replied mischievously. The impetigo had disappeared in a week.

The rum in water had worked wonders for Nic's cough but the day before Charlie's visit to the mad professor I had visited a pharmacist in Sliema who catered for English visitors, and bought a cough medicine which he recommended. It was pink and very sweet. The following day Nic had had his two hour nap and I was rummaging in a crate trying to find some toys whilst he was supposedly riding his little tricycle in the yard, but all was very quiet and I went to check. Soon bored he had gone into the house, climbed onto the table in the kitchen and managed to reach the door of the kitchen cupboard, where he knew his cough medicine was kept. Instead of a screw top the bottle had a cork inserted in the top, and I found him sitting on the table clutching a half empty bottle.

With no idea of what was in the pink concoction. I grabbed Nic and the bottle and ran to my landladies who, I knew, had a phone. The younger lady opened the door, barefoot, eyes half shut and glared at me as I gabbled "I am so sorry, but Nic has had an accident and Charles has the car. How do I get a taxi to take him to the hospital?"

I had obviously disturbed her afternoon nap. For a moment she stood open mouthed, then ran to fetch her sister who also came to the door, where they both threw their arms in the air, one shrieking "Ajjut!, ajjut!" and the other "Maria, Maria!" The younger sister ran into their living room and started shouting down the phone, whilst the older sister clasped Nic, now hiccupping and retching, to her very ample bosom as she exclaimed "The poor, poor child! It will come now!"

Almost immediately a taxi came trundling up the road

and I bundled us into an ancient Austin Seven car. "Is he very sick the poor child?" yelled the taxi driver over the noise of the engine in between yelling at other drivers, as he careered as fast as his old vehicle would allow down potholed streets and very narrow alleys.

"I don't know but please will you wait for us?" I begged as I ran into the now familiar hospital, imagining Nic having his stomach pumped out. A young nun, tiny and almost disappearing under her enormous wimple, came to us immediately. I handed the medicine bottle to her and pointed at Nic, trying to smile and explain what had happened, just as he wailed loudly and brought up a surprisingly large amount of pink vomit on to the beautiful tiled floor. Within a few minutes a very grumpy, elderly doctor, who had impeccable English, had assured me no stomach pump was necessary, given me a stern lecture that I should never leave medicines within reach of a child, and dismissed me with a wave of his immaculately manicured hand as he said "Please go to the office to provide your details and an address to which we should send the account."

It was then I realised I had dashed out of the house with no money! I had no idea where Charlie was, neither had I any idea how to get back home. Making sure I had tight hold of Nic's hand I stood in the road, too embarrassed to return to the taxi, but the driver saw us and came over. He was a middle aged man, rather plump and almost bald, and had a friendly face. He looked at Nic and asked "Alright?"

"Yes" I replied, "but I was so frightened I came out without any money!"

He grinned, put his hand in his pocket, gave me a shilling piece, and with an exaggerated wink said "That is for the bus!" and turned away before I could thank him. There was no bus in sight and I started to walk up the hill away from Sliema just as

Charlie suddenly appeared in the car.

"Our landlady is not as unfriendly as we thought" he explained. "She came rushing out the minute I got back from Valetta and told me what had happened, and I guessed you'd be back in the same hospital. I just hope we're not going to have much more Maltese medicine!"

EXPLORING

Away from Valetta and Sliema the roads were full of potholes with no verges or pavements whilst a heap of limestone blocks, piled up in the middle of nowhere, usually signalled the building of a new house. The edge of a road or track was often lined by prickly pear plants, their orange or red fruit enticing the foolhardy unaware of the almost invisible spines covering the tough leaves, whilst dust covered green-grey oleander trees occasionally broke up the monotonous landscape. Now September, the Island was completely parched and brown, but despite the heat men plodded behind donkey drawn ploughs in tiered fields which still yielded potatoes, tomatoes and beans, the soil heaped in little mounds around each individual plant to capture every drop of water.

At last mobile again, Charlie asked the foreman if he could suggest other places of interest to visit. "Of course, of course! You must visit the Victoria Lines to see how the British believed they would keep out the enemy!" and he laughed.

We made our way towards the north end of the Island, and stopped on a stony flat area overlooking the sea. We set off along a sandy pebbly path, where the only plants were ground hugging clumps of bushes, some vivid green, others a darker shade, the dry remains of flowers still hanging on. The rocky landscape hid small, unexpected valleys, or suddenly revealed a hill with an old lookout or fort slowly crumbling away in the hot wind.

We met no-one for the first half hour until a couple with a small fair haired boy appeared, coming towards us. Obviously not Maltese they stopped, the man saying "Hello, don't recognise you! Which Service are you in?" Thus started a life-long friendship with David and his wife Peggy, particularly since their little boy was also called 'Nicholas', and the boys were very close in age.

David was a naval officer and told us why, in the late nineteenth century, the British had built the Lines. Victorian military strategists had recognised that the 'Great Fault', a natural fissure which cuts across Malta from east to west, could be a line of defence if invaders landed on the North end of the Island. They built a defence system of walls, forts and gun positions, and although it was never tested, some of the walls and forts still stood.

"There are plenty of places to go and things to see on the Island" David said as we parted making arrangements to meet again, "and you must go to Dingli Cliffs! They're limestone and you'll find all kinds of fossils up there, which the experts say is proof that Africa and Europe were originally physically connected – and anyway it's always worth going because, from up there, you'll see one of the best seascapes anywhere in the world – and I've seen a few" he added, laughing as he drove away.

We decided to follow his suggestion and the next weekend we drove westwards across the Island, the rough, dusty roads getting narrower and narrower. Gradually climbing, we made our way through several apparently deserted villages past small shrines comprising a few colourless flowers draped over a faded plastic Madonna, some enclosed within a crumbling stone wall, others left on the roadside. Almost illegible, faded wooden signs leading to a church or an archaeological site had been driven into the hard ground every mile or so, and we realised we would never run out of places to visit.

Without warning the stony track ended at a makeshift car park. With nothing ahead but space and blue sky we stepped out onto shiny, smooth rock, all the soil long since blown away by the wind. With the Dingli cliffs rising nearly a thousand feet straight up from the sea, and with no fencing to prevent a plunge to certain death, we both held Nic in a firm grip as we gazed at the endless seascape. Still somewhat puzzled by David's enthusiasm for this isolated part of the Island we were nevertheless reduced to silent awe by the vast expanse of water disappearing into the horizon. The wind was light but very warm, the sea far, far below, pale blue, almost motionless.

"That must be Filfla" Charlie said pointing at a tiny island about three miles out to sea, "and that large rock near it is Filflaletta. It's been almost blown to bits by the navy and the air-force using it for bombing practice. The foreman told me that divers try to find bits of ordnance on the sea bed and use it for making their fireworks!"

"Good grief, how dangerous" I exclaimed, and feeling somewhat disorientated I turned to leave just as a flock of animals, half sheep, half goat, came into view. Wandering at will they were accompanied by a very small boy in ragged trousers and a stained, thin tee shirt, the skinny animals with spindly legs and very long ears nibbling furiously at the bare ground.

"It is a fantastic seascape, but I wonder what David was getting at?" Charlie wondered.

As we turned our backs on the sea we saw a large, unusual building nearby and wandered over. Built of limestone in the shape of a Latin cross, with no dome or spire it was obviously very old, and seriously in need of repair. A small plaque told us that, despite being hit by lightning in 1936, St. Mary Magdelene Chapel, the 'chapel of the cliffs', was the parish church for the local farmers and their families, who held a festa in August every year with the usual carrying of the statue of Our Lady.

Suddenly an unexpected gust of wind blew clouds of gritty dust into our faces.

"I wouldn't want to be carrying the statue up here if it was windy" Charlie exclaimed. "It'd be frightening in a storm! Come on, let's go." As we were making our leisurely way over the stony ground towards the car, a barrage of gun shots suddenly erupted on all sides.

"Quick, get to the car" Charlie shouted as he grabbed Nic. We ran back to the safety of the car at a gallop, threw him into the back seat and, with no-one to be seen, drove away as fast as my Morris Minor would go.

I felt rather shaky and we were both puzzled and uneasy. "Surely you shouldn't be shot at in the middle of the country!" I protested.

At the building site next day Charlie cornered the foreman and told him what had happened. "You were safe, it was nothing" he replied grinning broadly, but gave no explanation.

Many months later our Maltese friend Fred provided the answer. With no trace of embarrassment he explained " it is our sport! We shoot the birds as they fly between Africa and Europe each Autumn and again the following Spring. You were in no danger I assure you." It seemed the Maltese killed birds, ate birds and stuffed birds in huge numbers – obviously the reason why there were no seagulls!

Whenever I went to Sliema, I always drove past a replica of an English village church. A rather paltry building compared to the huge flamboyant Catholic churches, it appeared strangely out of place against the brilliant blue sky, and I decided to investigate. Once inside I was pounced on by an elderly gentleman who insisted on showing me round and telling me how the Anglican Church in Malta came about almost by accident. "In the mid-nineteenth century" he explained "Gibraltar had a well- established Anglican tradition with its own Bishop, the

Reverend William Trower. The English community in Sliema had no church to go to, and he successfully appealed for funds to buy land and build a church." He went on to tell me how it had been deliberately designed in the early English style with a pitched roof, as it was intended to remind sailors of the village churches they had left behind.

Holy Trinity Church was consecrated in 1867, and as I thanked him for a most informative tour he smiled and said "Now, shall I tell you the gossipy bit?" Apparently the Reverend Trower had three young daughters, Jane, Frances and Mary. Life in Sliema, then a village, was very quiet, so they abandoned the Bishop's House in Sliema and moved to the Bishop's Palace in Valetta where various Army Regiments and Queen Victoria's navy ensured that life in Valetta was a constant whirl of social events.

On one of her rare chatty days, our younger landlady told me about San Anton Palace. "It is a very grand place with beautiful gardens" she said "but it is a long way to go to Attard, and I have myself visited only once in my lifetime. You will find the history very interesting. Myself, I have no respect for those Knights, they had so many servants because they were very lazy!" she exclaimed.

"Let's go" I suggested one weekend, "but we better allow enough time because it's a long way " I repeated, forgetting we were in Malta – fifteen minutes, and all of four and a half miles later, tall palm trees swaying in the distance told us we were nearing the entrance to the Palace. A solitary policeman showed us where to park, and handed us a small booklet before we walked through crumbling pillars into the gardens. Originally built as a country villa for one of the Knights of the Order of St. John, it was later extended into a Palace with a tall tower and numerous shady courtyards. The standing army of soldier-monks, who took care of Christian pilgrims on their journey to Jerusalem, had been hounded out by the Turks, firstly from the

Holy Land to Cyprus and then to Rhodes and they were still in pursuit of the Christians. In 1530, in return for their military assistance in his fight against the infidel, the King of Spain provided the Knights with a sanctuary in Malta, and for the next two and a half centuries, under constant threat of invasion by the Turks, the Knights continued to argue and bicker about the best means of defending Malta.

Meanwhile their lavish lifestyle required cooks, food tasters, torch bearers, wig makers, physicians, and even a baker to make black bread to feed to their hunting dogs. Italian military engineers produced plan after plan to protect Valetta, Grand Harbour and the Three Cities, but because the Knights could never agree on any of them, the fortifications had still not been completed when Napoleon sailed into Grand Harbour in June 1798. In return for estates in France and pensions for the Knights, the Order had surrendered without a fight, and left the Island in disgrace.

The Palace was surrounded by trees, an oasis of peace and coolness and had had various uses, eventually becoming the residence for British Government officials and Governors-General.

Huge, vibrant pink bougainvillaea grew up the white walls of the building in glorious bursts of colour, whilst exotic plants, ornamental trees and immaculate flower beds blooming with orange, red and yellow annuals, were a delight.

I had to be dragged away to see the numerous ponds teeming with goldfish and an enormous peacock, strutting about, glaring at all the onlookers.

Nic was fascinated by the bird until it suddenly spread its magnificent turquoise tail and started to head towards us, making a horrible squawking noise.

"Go away, go away!" he yelled, jumping into his pushchair, and although we visited the Gardens several times, he would never again go anywhere near the peacock.

Early in October our exploring took us to Malta's original capital, Mdina, the Silent City. Founded by the Phoenicians around the eighth century, it had withstood sieges in the eleventh century and the fifteenth century, as well as an earthquake in 1693. When the Knights arrived they had established Birgu (later Vittoriosa) as their capital, replacing it with Valetta as the new capital after the Great Siege, but for the Catholic Church and Maltese aristocracy Mdina remained the true capital of Malta throughout the Middle Ages. The nobility passed their property down from one generation to the next, and when the twentieth century brought cars, lorries and buses to the Island only members of the aristocracy and the Church were issued with permits allowing them to drive a car into their city.

The weather was hot and sultry as we drove slowly up the steep hill from Mgarr towards the small, fortified town sitting on a rocky hill on the north-west side of the Island. As we drove past the city walls rising up from a deep, dry moat, thin veils of light cloud drifted past the massive dome of St. Paul's Cathedral towering over the edges of the fortifications, so that for a moment the ancient church almost disappeared, as if floating in a haze of smoke. We parked the car, and walked across an arched stone bridge over the moat which led to the Main Gate, a spectacular, monumental gateway adorned with the carved coat of Arms of the grand Master who had commissioned it.

In the centre of the gateway a tall narrow arch, guarded on either side by a large limestone lion, and wide enough only for a single karrozzin to trot through at any one time, led us into a silent, empty piazza. Cool and shadowy, a grey and white cat, padding slowly and unhindered across the wide, cobbled space, was the only proof of life going on in the small palaces which surrounded the square. No building in the ancient, baroque city was without its adornment of stone carvings, garlands, female figures, floral motifs, symbols of military warfare and other decorative sculptures, their shuttered windows and massive wooden doors protecting the inhabitants from the twentieth century.

Only seven miles separated the two capital cities, but in the eighteenth century a three hour journey to Valetta in a horse-drawn carriage, with dust filling every nook and cranny, was not for the faint-hearted. The grand ladies of Mdina had no choice but to stay at home in their magnificent houses and palaces, hoping to catch any tiny ripple of wind that might stir the otherwise motionless atmosphere in the gloomy, but relatively cooler, rooms. However, in the nineteenth century news of railways and closed train carriages arrived on the Island and a London firm of engineers was instructed to organise the building of a railway to connect the two capitals.

February 1883 saw the first olive green locomotives on black frames chugging across the Island from one capital to the other in only twenty five minutes, with wooden carriages on iron frames providing first and third class seats on both sides of an aisle, all illuminated with candles. At some stations trains going in both directions met, and a system of collection and distribution of post was devised by attaching metal boxes to the trains where letters could be posted, or collected, several times each day until the railway was closed in 1931.

On returning to the UK three years later I met my great-aunt who exclaimed "You must be so glad to be back in civilisation after three years! What on earth did you find to do to pass the time?"

I just smiled and replied "Plenty!"

A magnificent gateway

HOUSE HUNTING

After our cottage in the mountains of Snowdonia the tiny yard in the house in Sliema must have felt like a prison to Nic. He had no toys to play with, and in desperation we bought him a tricycle. For a couple of days it occupied him, whizzing from the kitchen into the sitting room, bumping into everything as he failed to make it round a corner, but he soon returned to his favourite indoor pastime - climbing onto the chairs and leaping across onto the settee. Fearing for the return of our deposit we decided to look for another home. Paul, who was Australian, and his English wife lived in a large, airy flat around the corner and suggested we tried to find somewhere similar. However our new naval friends told us that furnished villas were available in some of the villages for those who retired to live in Malta after leaving the Services, and for visitors who arrived for extended holidays. We decided to try to find somewhere with a garden.

I had assumed that all children with impetigo would be kept away from Nic, but discovered that no-one bothered about isolating the sufferers and, as our spots had almost disappeared, it seemed a good time to do some house hunting. Charlie needed the car to get to Marsa, so it meant I would have to travel to the various villages by bus.

"By bus!" exclaimed one of the younger Service wives at a coffee morning in a modern, beautifully furnished flat in Sliema to which a new acquaintance had kindly invited me. "You can't do that surely? You won't know which bus to catch and the villages are away from where the British live, with no shops or anything like that!" The chatter ceased as all the wives looked me up and down. I felt very foolish, and wished I had not mentioned that I was house-hunting.

"Well, nowhere is very far away on the Island is it? I can hardly get lost, and I've decided to start in the Three Villages, so I could always walk back if I had to" I replied, rather defiantly.

"You'll soon find out that everywhere is far away when you start walking in the heat" said a rather plump, blonde, older woman, with a grimace, "but good luck my dear. You must let us know how you get on," and she turned away.

The bus journeys were great fun for Nic, They acquainted me with The Three Villages, Attard, Balzan and Lija, and also gave me an insight as to how traffic behaved. Officially all vehicles drove on the left, but because there were few white lines marking the centre of the roads most buses and cars drove haphazardly wherever the driver chose - usually in the middle . Never giving any signals, and shooting out of side roads without glancing to right or left drivers appeared blissfully unaware that around any corner might appear a donkey pulling a wooden cart loaded with vegetation, rabbit hutches, pumpkins and, often, elderly women, or a flock of animals, half sheep, half goat, shepherded by young children, filling the narrow lane.

As the only form of public transport buses were everywhere, ancient, noisy and smelly, belching black smoke as they hurtled along, bumping in and out of potholes, squealing to a halt to avoid the odd goat ambling along the road. Sprayed a bright red, green or blue to indicate their route, a girl's name, some English (Mary and Gladys two of the favourites) others Maltese (such as Doris or Maria) was painted along the bonnet in old fashioned twirling script. Many drivers hung lace curtains and beads in the windows, whilst others propped vases of artificial flowers and a statue of the Virgin Mary on the dashboard.

I decided to go to Attard, where we had been told the housing was a mix of traditional two and three storey houses, and a few modern villas set in well maintained gardens. I strapped Nic in his pushchair and walked down to the main road. Several buses went past with no name of a destination at the front, merely a white card with a number on it stuck at the top of the windscreen. I had no idea which bus to get. I stood in the sun for about ten minutes and was very hot, and almost in despair, when a youngish woman joined me at the stop. Taking courage in both hands I smiled at her and asked "Attard?" She also smiled, and in perfect English replied "Ah, you need number 9. Attard is on the route to Rabat, but you must put your hand out to make sure the bus will stop. There will be one soon."

"Soon" became another twenty minutes before a very ancient vehicle came rattling slowly up the hill from Sliema. Terrified it would go past without stopping I waved my arm frantically as it maintained the same speed, whilst a bad tempered face peered at me through the open window of the cab. "Rabat?" grunted the driver as he passed me.

"Yes, yes, please!" I called out. "Please stop!"

He halted several yards away from the stop, turned the engine off, got out and went into a nearby shop. The bus had no door. I unstrapped Nic, placed him on the second stair, folded the pushchair, grabbed him as he tried to come back down the stairs and got him, the pushchair and myself inside, and we sank onto a sagging seat - objects of several pairs of curious eyes. Ten minutes passed until the driver jumped back on board, bowed his head to his statue, crossed himself twice (giving his passengers time to do likewise), restarted the engine, stuck a cigarette in his mouth, swung the steering wheel sharply to one side and tore off in the direction of the centre of the Island. Clinging on to the seat in front with one hand I frantically held on to Nic who was jumping up and down, laughing and clapping his hands, whilst the other passengers, all Maltese, joined in.

We had travelled no more than about four miles which took about an hour, as we stopped every half mile or so for plump young women each with two or three small children, or an old man with a rabbit in a box or a bird in a cage, got on or off, talking and laughing all the while.

I had no idea where Attard was but again was rescued by a fellow traveller. "Attard please?"I asked a lady sitting opposite me.

She flashed a smile and turned to her companion who replied "not yet. I will tell you" - which she did, when we eventually arrived in a square and stopped opposite a Church.

When I had set off the heat was manageable but now, at almost midday, the sun was beating down. Siesta time, there was no-one about. With no shade from the buildings I made my way through the deserted village following the map the agent had provided, feeling utterly foolish as I recalled the warning the plump naval wife had given me. At last I found the address, obviously a modern property, and by now I was so hot and dishevelled I knew I looked a mess in my blouse and shorts and flip flops.

The garden was still colourful and green despite the heat, hibiscus bushes lining the short pathway to the house, all of which signalled "water - expensive". The door was opened by a very glamorous Maltese woman in a tailored dress, high heels, gold earrings and bangles, her hair and makeup perfect. She smiled graciously and I felt even more awkward as she invited me in. We entered a cool space lavishly furnished, with arrangements of real flowers on glass tables and an antique piano gleaming with polish in pride of place in the lounge. Holding him tightly in my sweaty hand, Nic and I walked behind the lady into the lounge as she said "Mrs. Corke, maybe you play the piano? If so, this house would be interesting to you I believe?"

"Occasionally" I replied in awe of her and the house.

"Good! Shall we proceed to the new kitchen?" As we turned away Nic pulled free of my slippery grip and darted over to the piano. Smiling happily he cried "Look, like Nain's house!" lifted the lid and started hitting the keys - only to reveal that it was hopelessly out of tune! Aghast, I grabbed hold of him, mumbled my excuses and made a dash to the door, leaving a very embarrassed lady behind.

Almost in tears I strapped Nic back in his pushchair, found my way back to the square and sat on a bench outside the Church in a tiny strip of shade. Hotter than ever I realised I had brought nothing to drink (I never did that again) just as a man pushing a cart of bread and vegetables came round the corner and stopped near me, pulling a bottle of Cisk out from a basket slung under the cart. I took my purse from my bag, waved it at him and called Cisk? Grinning he pulled two more bottles of beer out of the basket as the bus came into view, and giving him most of my loose change I clambered on board, opened one bottle, gave Nic a long drink and before I had finished the remainder he was asleep on my knee. The second bottle restored my equilibrium as we trundled back to Sliema, and for once I was delighted to see our ugly little house.

"I don't want to go viewing any more places" I announced rather pathetically as I recounted my adventure to Charlie, who roared with laughter.

"Well, if you don't want to stay here for two years we'll have to do something" he replied. "Paul has seen an advert for a place in St. Julian's that sounds interesting and we can go and view it at the weekend."

The house was by the sea, and had a boathouse. The living room opened onto a terrace overlooking the little harbour where several luzzu were bobbing about in the sparkling, blue water. It also had a sun room and seemed idyllic until we saw the tiny third bedroom so, hoping to have many visitors, we decided the house was too small.

After several bus journeys, and viewing about ten places with no success, I was getting desperate until, in the middle of October, Charlie came home with details of two possible houses. A very old villa in Sliema with a shady courtyard and two gardens seemed a real possibility, but the arrangement of the rooms was very peculiar so we decided against it.

"I don't think we're ever going to find somewhere with a garden" I said despondently.

"Cheer up" Charlie replied. "I know the other house is not by the sea, but let's go and have a look at it."

DECISION TIME

The other house was in one of the traditional villages, off Valley Road on the main route to Mdina.

As we approached Birkirkara my first impression was of tall spires and glistening domes cluttering the sky line. Reputedly there are more than seven hundred Catholic churches in Malta and Gozo, an average of about one church per square kilometre. Flamboyant churches, creamy- white limestone walls flaking and fading in the hot Mediterranean sun, constantly reminded me that the Maltese and Gozitan people are very devotional. Religious festivals, the tolling of bells, and the sound of exploding fireworks from near and far, quickly became part of our daily lives, and there could have been no more dramatic a change from North Wales with its rain washed grey, stone chapels and stern, non-conformist traditions.

It appeared Birkirkara had more than its fair share. Amongst others, St. Roque's Church was built in 1593, closed then rebuilt in 1676 after the plague had swept through the islands, whilst Santa Maria Church was built in 1679 on a hill, safe from attack by corsairs. In Birkirkara a large grand basilica had been built in the baroque style, inspired by Mdina Cathedral, and consecrated in 1745. Dedicated to St. Helen, it had the largest church bell in Malta.

On the phone the letting agent had told Charlie that the villa was close to the Church of St Francis in Msida Street, "and" he added mysteriously "it has a history that will be interesting to you I am sure." It transpired that in June 1940 a community of Franciscan Friars had been evacuated from Valetta to a villa in Birkirkara, which they used as a temporary church until the end of the War. The owner of the villa had bought land in Birkirkara to build a modern church nearby to be dedicated to St. Francis of Assisi, and he also owned two other villas, one of which we had come to view.

We turned off Valley Road into a narrow, shadowy street overhung with balconies, each in turn overhung with washing. The soft limestone, constantly shedding small flakes and gritty fragments onto the roadway, gave the houses a worn and shabby appearance, and my first impression was of a rather neglected area. "Oh no, not another fool's errand" I muttered.

"Yes, it doesn't look very promising" Charlie agreed, but the road suddenly widened out with small one storey houses on one side and two large houses on the other. "Never mind, we'll just have a quick look at the place – we'll have to, because there's somebody waiting for us."

A smartly dressed middle aged man was standing by a gate, which he opened with a dramatic flourish as he exclaimed "Mr. and Mrs. Corke, may I welcome you to Birkirkara, not forgetting of course this young man" as he patted Nic on the head. "You will notice that originally there was one large house, which has been divided into two. Come, please, and you will see how successfully this has been achieved."

As Charlie and Nic followed the agent I stood back and enjoyed my first impression of the villa. Here, at last, was a lovely old house, set above the road with steps going up to a stone terrace that ran across the front of the building, part of a single storey addition to the villa. A typical Maltese front door, windowless, made of solid wood and painted a dull green, opened into a very large hallway, a door on the left leading to a big room furnished as a dining room, and on the right to a cloakroom. A couple of yards beyond the cloakroom another door opened into a lounge with french windows onto the garden. About thirty feet long, it was again fully furnished, with a selection of various chairs and sofas, foot rests and small tables, and two old fashioned drinks cupboards. At the far end of the hallway a wide, sweeping staircase, with an ornamental metal balustrade, disappeared into semi-darkness above. At the side of the staircase the hall narrowed into a passageway with a door off it into a medium size room behind the lounge, again with french windows into the garden, empty apart from an old cupboard and a couple of chairs. A door at the end of the hall led into a big square kitchen, with a scullery beyond, then another small room beyond which was a toilet, and at last a back door, again giving access to the garden.

The staircase led to a small landing with a window overlooking the garden. Three doors opened off it, on the right side into a spacious bedroom, another into the bathroom, and on the opposite side we saw an even larger bedroom, with a door at the opposite end into a smaller bedroom, perfect for Nic, which then led into another very small room. A spiral staircase in the corner of the largest bedroom gave access onto the roof and yet another small bedroom. All the rooms were furnished and the beds had new mattresses and pillows, as well as enormous, dusty mosquito nets hanging from the ceilings. With high ceilings, faded tiled floors throughout, green shutters on all the windows, and everywhere painted white, the house would always be cool and restful with no need for unreliable electric fans whirling the hot, dry air around. As the agent led us from room to room at a gallop I immediately felt comfortable, as if the house was welcoming us, but assumed it would be far too expensive. Lastly, he insisted that we went up to the roof to show us the water tanks, where washing lines were strung, criss-crossed like an enormous cat's cradle, enough to accommodate all the washing for a small hotel.

Back on the ground floor we stood in the hallway in silence, Charlie holding Nic firmly by the hand as the agent said "Mr. & Mrs. Corke, please accompany me to the garden. For the little boy it will provide much space for him to play." That was something of an understatement.

Running up the side of the house, and beyond it, was a huge walled garden in three sections. On a gentle incline, a central path divided each section with stone steps leading from one level to the next. Opposite the lounge french windows a very large pond, with a female - figure on a plinth in the middle, was overshadowed by a massive, dark pink bougainvillea growing up the garden wall, whilst lemon and orange trees were planted at regular intervals up each side of the central path. I stared in disbelief at this oasis of calm and beauty, and I knew without asking him that Charlie was as entranced as I was, and that this would be our home for the duration of the job, whatever it cost. In a daze I heard him ask, "What are the terms on which we could rent this house for two years?"

The agent beamed, and so did we, when he replied "The rent is twenty five pounds for each month, but you must agree to allow the gardener to look after the lemon and orange trees, and he will come as necessary for the good of the trees – you understand?"

"That's no problem. He can come whenever he wishes. How does he get into the garden?" asked Charlie.

"Of course, of course! You will see there is a small door in the wall by the roadside and he has a key. He has looked after the trees for many, many years for the owner and his family. Please, we must now make the legal contract as soon as possible. I will see you at my office in Valetta?"

Our oasis of peace and beauty

Delighted with our find we agreed to take it from the 1st November 1963, despite having to also pay for the other house for the weeks that remained under our first contract. There was no garage, but we decided that as my Morris Minor was quite old it would be fine parked in the road outside our gate.

Charlie went to Valetta after taking us back home where I found a letter lying behind the door. It was from my mother. She would be arriving on Sunday the 3rd November 1963 on an overnight flight from London "to keep my promise to come as soon as you were settled."

"Nic, guess what? Nain's coming to see us very soon. Won't that be lovely for you?" I exclaimed.

He stopped halfway through his jumping-off-the-furniture game, stared at me for a moment and then, clapping his hands, cried "Nain in an aeroplane soon? " and ran to the yard to get his tricycle.

A letter went back by return warning her that she would be coming to a place where some essential pieces of equipment would possibly not be working, unpacked boxes and tea chests would be scattered about the house - and the humidity would be at its worst.

BIRKIRKARA

A week before we moved to the villa Charlie went to work with Paul and I spent a morning finding my way about in Birkirkara. I parked the car by the gate of our future home and set off towards the square.

Meandering along I came across a very old architectural structure which (I was later to discover) was a length of the Wignacourt Aqueduct. Built by the Knights in 1615 to bring water from the springs in Dingli and Rabat on the west side of the island to the newly built Valetta, much of the water was carried through underground pipes, but where there were depressions in the ground or small valleys they built lengths of arched viaducts, one of which I had found. The ancient cisterns under the city, all the ships in the harbours, and the population of over thirty thousand souls received their supply of fresh water from the other side of the Island.

"How on earth is so much of the viaduct still standing?" I asked Charlie that evening.

"No idea. I'll have to find out" he replied. The following day he told me the site foreman had explained that the stone arches had been bonded using pozzolana, a mixture of volcanic ash and quick lime. Discovered by the Greeks about 500BC, the Romans added salt water to the mix, which made it even stronger, "and that is why so many ancient buildings have survived centuries of wind and weather" he finished.

A large village, Birkirkara sprawled untidily on either side of a valley which flooded during the winter storms – hence its name which means 'a place of running water.' Originally a small settlement, when the Knights arrived they had immediately built a church, and over the centuries more houses had sprung up haphazardly, different heights and different widths, creating dark narrow alleyways, always leading to and from the Church. Judging by the smiles and waves as I negotiated the narrow alleys the local bush telegraph had been very busy, and a troop of little boys trailed behind us, one on either side of the pushchair holding Nic's hands.

Reminders of British rule were everywhere – red letter boxes, rubbish collected twice every day, milk delivered before dawn and again late afternoon, a photograph of the Queen and Prince Philip pinned to the wall by the open door to the Police Station.

We knew there were no blocks of flats for Service families in the village, and no Service families meant no shops as we knew them. As I was making my way back to the car "Lady, lady, you want bread?" one little boy asked eagerly. "Here there is a shop." A curtain of multi coloured plastic strips flapping over the open door of a building not far from the villa was the only indication of a shop inside. Out of the brilliant sunshine the shop was very dark and I could just make out a large electric fan whirring in one corner, a cat snoozing on an upturned box nearby, and a stout lady with an apron tied round her middle sitting behind a makeshift counter, bouncing a baby on her knee. Piles of flat loaves, large tubes of tomato paste, a few sad-looking vegetables, mostly unidentifiable limp green leaves, tomatoes and potatoes, a pile of pomegranates, powdered milk and tins of fish and corned beef seemed to be the main items I would find in these establishments. On the floor cages of various sizes were stacked one on top of the other, many containing small birds singing their hearts out in the gloom, others containing rabbits crouching and twitching in terror awaiting their certain fate. I bought a couple of pomegranates and some tomatoes, whilst sticky sweets were pressed into Nic's eager little hands by the owner as she said "Goodbye, goodbye. I shall see you again madam?" and I nodded and smiled in reply.

As I walked I observed my future neighbours. They moved slowly whatever their task. The older men wore shabby flat caps, baggy trousers and thin cotton shirts, sleeves rolled up to show sinewy arms, bare, brown feet thrust into old leather sandals. The younger men were often on the plump side with smart haircuts, tidy clothes and large, flashy wrist watches, and seemed to spend their time hanging round the bars, cigarette in hand, laughing and calling out to passers-by, occasionally holding the hand of a small child. The women were bareheaded, never without glittering gold earrings, the younger ones pretty with black wavy hair and beautiful teeth, dressed simply in cotton frocks and flip-flops, usually with very young children in tow, whilst the older women were replicas of the lady I met in the grocers shop.

I returned to Sliema, assured that our neighbours would be friendly and kind, and a few days later, before we moved to the villa, Charlie announced over supper "We've got to have a maid."

I stared at him. "A maid! What kind of maid?"

"One of the foremen on the site asked me if we already had a maid because he knows of a very nice girl living in the village, not far from the big Church. He says she is really good with children and is old enough to work as she is sixteen."

"I don't need a maid" I protested, typically having given no thought as to how I was going to keep the huge villa clean.

"Jan" he replied, "if we have a maid it's a way the British help the economy because there's no other work, especially for girls when they leave school. Anyway, have you thought about the size of the villa?"

Recalling the friendliness I had encountered on my walk through the village any misgivings I had expressed immediately vanished, and as soon as we moved to our new home Doris became an indispensable part of our family for the next three years. However, rather strangely, apart from the couple who lived in the next door villa we were the only British people who lived in Birkirkara - as far as I ever discovered.

OUR NEW HOME

On the first of November 1963 we arrived at the villa early on the Friday morning, to find the agent standing by the front door. He wasted no time. After shaking our hands he handed Charlie a huge bunch of keys saying "You are an engineer Mr. Corke, so you will need no explanations from me as to how things work."

Throwing open the french windows in the lounge he continued "of course, as you know the villa has been empty for some time but soon it will be a home from home for you all. I also live in this town and know that all your neighbours are good people. I wish you much happiness during your stay on our Island. Goodbye" and he ran down the front steps, through the gate and was gone.

As the metal gate clanged shut I looked at Charlie. "Oh lord, what on earth have we done?" I grimaced, staring at the keys.

"Well, we're stuck with it now!" was his unhelpful reply. "I'd better try and find out which key fits which lock before bedtime."

As the agent drove off in his large, but ancient, car an even older lorry came rumbling up the lane from the main road and stopped by our gate. Two young men jumped out, ran to the back, off loaded our crates, ran up the steps, dumped them in the hallway, shouted what sounded like "lx-Xorti", ran back to the lorry and disappeared into the village.

Our village

"What were they saying?" I asked.

"I've no idea" replied Charlie. "Come on, we've so much to do – and where's Nic?"

"I've no idea either!" A sudden thought hit me. "Charlie, Mum's arriving in two days – how am I going to get out and about to show her the Island?" He would now need the car to get to work – could I get onto the buses with a toddler and a parent?

"I'll think of something" he called as he ran up the steps. On Monday he bought a third hand scooter which was very cheap, cost almost nothing to run, and the problem was solved.

Charlie's answer to most problems was a cup of tea and I

had brought a packet of tea, a carton of milk and a small tin of sugar with me. He went in search of the mains water stop-cock, and as soon as he shouted "water's on" I went into the kitchen where I met the other permanent resident, a gecko, which lived somewhere at the back of the villa and visited us every day. We never discovered where he lived but would suddenly catch sight of a movement on the wall, usually above the cooker, where he stayed inert for several minutes, then was gone.

I watched him as water dribbled reluctantly out of a large, old fashioned tap, eventually filling the kettle. I found cups and a teapot and, after exploring the back of the house, realised that the kettle had still not come to the boil. Recalling the vagaries of the electricity supply, we soon remembered never to turn on more than three lights when using the cooker or the immersion heater, and got used to the kettle taking ten minutes to come to the boil, the lights suddenly going dim, and the television regularly fading for a few minutes.

Rented out for several years, everything in the house was rather dated and well-used. In the kitchen a big wooden table sat squarely in the middle surrounded by a collection of hard, upright plastic chairs. A large, old fashioned cupboard, with two drawers still full of odds and ends, contained pots, pans, tableware and cutlery and, curiously, stacks of airtight tins. I soon discovered why. Not only was the weather hot, the humidity was often greater than the heat and flour was a prime target for weevils. Coffee and sugar went rock hard within a couple of days, and biscuits and cereals became soggy immediately they were opened, even when stored in the tins. A fairly modern electric cooker and a large fridge looked promising, and in the scullery a huge stone sink with the cold tap and a wooden draining board completed the equipment.

My mother's imminent arrival was our first challenge. "What had we better do first?" asked Charlie as we supped our tea.

"Mum will have been travelling for about twenty four hours so I must make sure she's got a bed to fall into straight away" I replied. "Trouble is, I can't remember what's in which packing case. I should have marked them before we left, but everything was such a rush."

Water was so expensive that meters were installed in all rented houses, and Charlie had immediately noticed that the tap in the scullery was dripping. "I better check if water's being wasted anywhere else" he said and soon returned with the bad news. Some taps produced no water because of rust in the pipes, two of the three lavatories were leaking, and when Charlie had turned on the main stopcock (rather strangely situated in a corner of the lounge) it had, unbeknown to us, started dripping.

Meanwhile, as I surveyed the crates and boxes in the hall shouts of "beach, beach!" stopped me in my tracks as Nic appeared by the french windows in the lounge. In the pond numerous, beautiful, large goldfish swam round and round, the sun's rays flickering on their scales as they surfaced from time to time, and the water was about two feet deep.

"I been swimming with the fishes" he said happily, standing in a large puddle after trailing water across the room. "You can come too?"

The need to find clothes bedding and towels was urgent. I chose a box at random and, finding a sharp knife in the kitchen, broke it open only to find it contained books. I spent the rest of the morning opening one container after another until suddenly it was lunch time. "We've no food in the house" I shouted from upstairs. "Quick, it's nearly twelve, and everyone shuts their shop at twelve!" Charlie ran to the little grocers arriving just as the lady I had met was locking her door, but she kindly let him in long enough to buy a loaf, a tube of tomato paste and a tin of sardines which, washed down with salty tap water, completed our first meal in the villa.

Clearly the next essential task was a trip to the supermarket in Sliema. Charlie hated shopping but announced he would go because "if you go, you'll wander round for ages, whereas I'll get what's on the list and come straight back" he said, quite correctly, and left the house with a long list including meat, fish, milk and other perishables.

I went to the kitchen to turn the big fridge on high, ready to store the goods on his return. It was very impressive at first sight, but I couldn't find any way of turning it on. Two hours later Charlie returned laden with several bags of food. "How I loathe shopping!" he exclaimed. "Never mind, we're well stocked for a week, and I even managed to get some decent wine!"

"Great" I said, "but I couldn't get the fridge to turn on." Dismayed we surveyed the shopping. The frozen meat and tuna steaks were already softening in their plastic containers, whilst the layers of news-paper, wrapped round the large tub of ice-cream to insulate it for the journey, were damp and starting to fray. Charlie said grimly "I'll go next door and see if they've got any spare space in their fridge —can't think of anything else can you?" and dashed off. He was back in a few minutes.

"Nice couple next door. No problem. They said bring the meat, fish and ice cream straight away and we can discuss things later" and disappeared with all the perishables. Mr. and Mrs. Next Door (they never told us their names) had kindly agreed, saying there was no hurry as they had plenty of spare capacity.

As soon as he returned Charlie inspected the fridge. "How did you try to turn it on?"

"That's just it - I couldn't find a plug or a socket."

"You never would" and he grinned. "It's an absorbtion refrigerator. It works on paraffin. Good grief, I never thought I'd see one of these again! It probably needs a good clean and a new wick." We knew all about such appliances because we had used paraffin heaters and lamps at the cottage. "Blow it, I'll have to go back to Sliema."

Whilst he was gone I filled the big sink with cold water, stood the three bottles of milk in it and phoned the agent. "Mrs. Corke, please accept my sincere apologies. I will see to it immediately, next week at the earliest!"

Having found bedding I made up the beds and attacked another crate containing Nic's toys, books and clothes, arranging them in the little bedroom in a way that I hoped would remind him of his room in the cottage. Charlie returned an hour later, hot but triumphant. "I found a shop selling all sorts of stuff for the house including paraffin fridges, new rubber washers for the dripping taps, a solution to deal with the clogged up taps, and other plumbing bits and pieces - and some strong netting to cover the pond. I'll clean the fridge and change the wick - won't take me long."

Half an hour later he re-appeared, very disgruntled. "I've done everything I can think of but nothing's happened. I'll have to ring the agent." Meanwhile, I tackled more crates and boxes, finding things we had not realised we had packed, and failing to find other things that we needed but had not packed and, by now late afternoon, I had a mild panic. There was so much to do and so little time to do it in before my mother arrived. Fortunately the cooker did work, and that evening we sat at the big table in the kitchen and had our first proper meal in our new home, but this time washed down with a Cisk for us and coke for Nic.

He had spent the day tearing from room to room on his tricycle, and running in and out of the french windows into the garden. I tried to settle him to sleep in his new bedroom under his small mosquito net, but the light didn't work and he refused to go to bed in the dark until I sat with him, fuming because we had so much to do. At last he was asleep and I went downstairs to the lounge to tackle another crate. Long curtains by the windows billowed into the room announcing a sudden, strong wind, accompanied by the intermittent patter of heavy rain drops. Trying to make some order out of the chaos we had forgotten to put the hood up on my precious Morris Minor before it went dark. In a panic I called "Charlie, Charlie where are you? There's going to be a storm! The car will be soaked!"

"I'm here!" he shouted crossly. "Couldn't you see me?" as he crawled from behind the sofa at the far end of the lounge. "The stopcock is dripping and I've just found water all over the floor. I could kill that agent – he hadn't checked anything, but it'll have to wait till we've covered the car."

We knew that changes in the weather raised the humidity level, and that when it was very high the hood shrank by about half an inch as the air temperature cooled. The downpour hit us as we ran down the steps and, wet through, we struggled and heaved on the roof pulling it in all directions, but it was hopeless.

"I saw some string in the kitchen drawer. I'll get that and you find some towels to put on the seats" Charlie shouted above the noise of the rain. It was the best we could do as we fought with the hood until, at last, we manged to tie it down to the windows of the car - and to my relief the road was deserted!

Back in the house, still sorting out the plumbing, Charlie fitted a new washer on the stopcock, and then covered the pond with the strong netting where, to his dismay, he found several unfortunate goldfish well and truly squashed lying at the bottom of the pond. I boiled the kettle, found more towels to dry ourselves, and after a hot drink we crawled under the mosquito net. "Just hope Nic doesn't wake early" I mumbled as sleep overtook me.

Trying to tidy up!

Next morning, as light squeezed through the slats in the shutters a little figure stood by the bed pulling at the mosquito net, and our day had begun. Chaos greeted us as we made our way down the sweeping staircase, and Saturday was spent trying to find homes for all our belongings and tidying the house ready for our visitor. At midnight we could do no more and slept so soundly that at eight on Sunday morning we were all still asleep.

My mother's flight was due in at nine and we drove furiously across the Island, Nic sitting on my knee, Charlie saying "Don't worry, these flights are never on time" only to see the regular BEA overnight flight from London approaching the airport. By the time we turned through the gates at Luqa it was taxiing up to the reception area, and grabbing Nic I raced up to the grandly named 'Viewing Gallery' just in time to see my mother getting off the plane.

NAIN'S VISIT

Her excitement and delight about her visit was revealed in a letter she wrote to Grandpa and Grandma on the 7th November 1963. She had flown before, but they had not and were very apprehensive, but nevertheless determined to come on a visit. She wrote "..............The journey was very enjoyable...the aircraft was a huge thing......I had a seat by the window. The windows in the Vanguard are the best windows in any aircraft as they are quite big...the seats are most comfortable as they will tip back.....luckily it was a lovely night, nearly a full moon and I could see the outline of the enormous wing and part of the tail of the aircraft and then when I looked down – the lights! Simply marvellous – Brighton was a mass of lights, different colours, and then we were over the channel, flying over the coast of France......and then all the lights down below again and a faint outline of the bridges when we were over Paris, then over Switzerland -Berne – the Alps, then the lights were dimmed.........and we were flying higher right up above the clouds.........a blanket of white clouds like a vast expanse of snow stretching as far as the eye could see.....I could not sleep........... I am sure you will find flying a most exciting experience!"

I never discovered how she persuaded my father to let her come alone, but we were delighted she had decided to visit us so soon. A devout Catholic country no form of family planning was available from a doctor or chemist in Malta, and we knew that tucked amongst her clothes were sufficient packets of the 'pill' to last us for twelve months.

"Are they very strict at the airport, going through your luggage?" she had asked in a letter.

"We don't really know" I had replied, but guessed that if found in my mother's luggage we could have been in serious trouble.

"They'll think I am just an innocent old lady (she was actually in her mid - fifties) and they'll never think of searching me or my luggage" she laughed, and fortunately she was right, but I was very relieved when she was safely in the car and away from the airport.

"I'll tell you want else I'm bringing with me" she had added in her letter "my paints and brushes and some good paper. There must be so many boats and buildings just waiting to be painted instead of my usual mountains – I can't wait!"

The first night she shared the spare bedroom with a family of mice. We did not even know they were there until she came down on the first morning. "How did you sleep? You must have been exhausted!" I said.

"I went off straight away, but I was a bit puzzled when I woke to go to the loo" she replied.

"What about?"

"I couldn't make out why those long curtains were rippling up and down because the windows were closed. Anyway I just got back into bed, but I looked this morning and saw several mice racing up and down!"

I was mortified. "Oh Mum you've come all this way, and then have mice in your bedroom! I'm so sorry – I'll go to Sliema straight after breakfast and try to find some mousetraps."

"Oh don't worry" she replied, "but I'm surprised you

didn't hear them squeaking in the night!" After catching two in our hastily obtained traps the survivors disappeared and never returned.

Before going to work, Charlie said "I've phoned the agent and told him I've done the repairs, but I want his plumbers to check."

"What did he say?" I asked.

Charlie grinned. "He said 'Mr.Corke, please accept my sincere apologies. Water wastage must not be allowed to happen. I will arrange everything immediately.' We'll see what happens!"

Later that morning two men arrived to "fix the fridge" - and immediately turned it upside down. "Madam, many fridges refuse to work if they have not been working for many years. Soon this will be fixed."

Two hours later, and after several such procedures, they had a long conversation, turned their hands palm upwards, shrugged their shoulders and prepared to leave. "Madam, I regret this machine will not work, and we must return to Valetta and inform the agent. Thank you goodbye" and they were gone. Several phone calls later a brand new Electrolux fridge arrived, and when I went to retrieve our food Mr. Next Door laughed and said "Ah yes, that's always their solution!"

Another three days passed before two plumbers arrived, but without their tools. They inspected everything but said they must return. Next day they came with hand tools but no ladder to get up to the tank and promised to return the next day with a ladder, but arrived without one. Nevertheless they went onto the roof, reappeared after an hour, said "all is now working", gave me a card with their details saying "for you madam, for the future" and left, smiling happily – they knew they would be back!

Nic was overjoyed to see his grandmother, and every morning settled into her bed where they had breakfast together and she told him stories about "home", and spent hours playing with him or reading books and teaching him nursery rhymes - that is when she was not helping me make loose covers. The three piece suite in the lounge was a dull, yellow colour and well used. The Maltese were very keen on buying material and making everything from clothes to curtains and soft furnishings. Material came from the UK as 'seconds' called 'fents', and sold by weight, the market in Valetta having rows of stalls loaded with rolls of good quality 'Grafton' cotton. After signing the tenancy agreement we had bought enough material to cover the suite and curtains to match.

"Your mother used to make your clothes during the War didn't she? I am going to ask her if she'll help you make some loose covers for the suite, unless you think you can manage without any help" Charlie said innocently, because we both knew I would be hopeless at such a task on my own. She fell into the trap and readily, and enthusiastically, agreed whilst he, ever the optimist, reckoned (and hoped) the job could be finished before she left. A random pattern of large multi-coloured flowers on a dark blue background meant that no careful matching of straight lines or edges was required, and after cutting the material into lengths he devised a way of folding the pieces, slip stitching the folds and finally tucking the material into the sides of the chairs and the sofa, rather than sewing the pieces together. His idea worked, and the loose covers were finished before she left three weeks later.

A few days after she arrived, as we were sitting in the lounge having a coffee break from our sewing, my mother said "Oh look, there's someone wandering about the garden. Who is it?"

Through the french windows we saw a very old man leaning on a stick in the shade of one of the trees. He wore baggy, almost ragged trousers, leather sandals secured with dirty string instead of a buckle on one side, a piece of material slung over his shoulder, and a cloth cap, possibly once white but now a brownish grey colour.

He slowly walked up to a small, stone shed at the top of the garden, unlocked it, took out a battered watering can and filled it from a tap nearby. He then retrieved a small hoe from the shed, returned to the paved central path, and walked slowly along gently loosening the soil around the base of the trunk of each fruit tree. He then filled each small trench with half a can of water, returned the tools to the stone shed, walked slowly back to the wooden door and disappeared.

"Well, that's interesting." I said. "I haven't seen him before, but he's supposed to come regularly."

"I wonder what else is in that stone shed?" she mused. "How can we find out?"

"No idea" I replied.

That afternoon, we set off to visit St. Helen's Basilica just as the gardener happened to walk past. "I wonder if my neighbour knows" I said, and embarked on a somewhat fragmented conversation with the Maltese lady across the road, busy wiping dust off her front door.

"Good day" I started.

"Good day Mrs. Corke" and she smiled at my mother and patted Nic on the head. "This lady is your visitor? Good day to you madam, and the little boy is well and not too hot?"

"Yes thank you, but can you tell me about the little house in the garden for looking after the trees?" I asked, hoping that by connecting the trees to the shed, she would understand my query, whilst my mother was clearly baffled by my weird manner of speech.

"Ah!" my neighbour replied "that little stone house – yes,

that was the other way to their house in the ground, for the war you see," and chucking Nic under the chin she said "Goodbye Mrs. Corke and madam" and disappeared through her plastic strip curtain, leaving us both even more baffled than before.

I decided to introduce my mother to some of our new friends. Charlie and I had met in an amateur dramatics society in North Wales, and whilst still living in Sliema I found a Methodist Church in Floriana where they ran such a society. We both joined, and Charlie was immediately roped in to make sets and deal with the electrics and I was cast in a play, a comedy that was to be staged before Christmas. Initially, because we had no babysitter, we took turns to attend rehearsals, but the arrival of Doris changed all that and I took my mother with me to the rehearsals, where our new friends quickly made her feel welcome.

Two days before the first performance I developed laryngitis, and turned up for the last rehearsal with a whisper. Everyone was aghast until an older man who had lived in the Island for years called out from the auditorium where he was arranging the seats. "Hot rum! That'll sort it out for you! Three or four times a day at least!" I had never tasted the mixture when we gave it to Nic, but after dosing myself at least four times a day, my voice recovered as I floated through each day in a haze. With little else by way of entertainment in November the audience (mostly Services personnel) were very appreciative and, because we had more room than anyone else, the "after play" party ended up in our house.

"What a party! I've not had such a good time in ages!" was Nain's verdict. "Service people certainly know how to have a good time!"

MUSHROOMS

I took my mother all over the Island despite her anxiety about the drivers, the potholed roads and lanes suddenly crowded with sheep and goats, but no other event or visit matched the cellar experience.

A few days after she arrived we were sitting in the kitchen having lunch when she suggested "I've been thinking - the smaller room through there has french windows onto the garden. What about moving your dining room into there and that big room opposite the lounge could be a play room for Nic." It was a good idea and when Charlie returned he agreed. The old cupboard had to be moved, and it took much heaving and grunting by Charlie before we heard the cupboard slide along the tiled floor.

A long silence followed, then "Jan, come and look at this" he called. He was examining a large wooden door set in the wall which backed on to the hallway. The metal handle was very rusty, but when he pressed it down the door immediately swung open revealing a space with a tiled floor, the size of a very small room.

He stepped inside, and running his hand over the wall by the side of the door found a switch and pressed it. The space immediately lit up, revealing a ventilation hole in one wall, and a trap door in the floor with a metal ring in it, obviously intended to give access to somewhere.

Traffic hazard

"I'll have to see what's under there – must be some kind of cellar" said Charlie heaving at the metal ring. The trap door resisted his efforts for a while, but suddenly jerked open allowing musty, dusty, wafts of air into the cupboard. Holding onto each other my mother and I peered down into a large space, faintly illuminated by the light in the room.

"What do we do now?" I asked, suddenly horrified by thoughts of dead bodies or stolen goods lying undiscovered under our dining room. Presumably our landlord had not wanted us to know of the secret room so after closing the trapdoor, and the door in the wall, Charlie decided to wander over the road to another of our Maltese neighbours, as usual sitting on a hard chair by his front door, smoking and chatting to passers-by.

"Good evening." he started.

"Mr. Corke, how are you and your family? I hope you are well, and that you are enjoying the beautiful house." As usual the formal manner of conversation was not easy to keep going, so Charlie plunged right in.

"We have found a door in the wall of one of the rooms and a hole in the floor inside a cupboard. Do you know what it is?"

Our neighbour grinned and replied "Mr. Corke, it is after the War. I will come with you and show you." He rose slowly, went into his house and emerged wearing his jacket and a cap – obviously it was to be a formal visit.

In the hallway he stopped, and removing his cap said "Mr. Corke, Mrs. Corke, and you madam (bowing slightly towards my mother) I remember this house very well. The same family have been the owners for many years, and the good Doctor has done much to help us all. Yes, the secret room. Please come." He walked towards the back of the house, stopped in the hallway before the door into the future dining room and rested his hand on the blank wall. "Mr. Corke, please put your hand by mine."

As Charlie did so he could feel a slight unevenness in the plaster as the old gentleman continued "Now we go into the room and you will see a door in the same position in that wall inside the room, and you will understand why there is a hole in the floor." He paused, smiled, tapped his forefinger against his nose and said "the good Doctor and his family had this secret, as I will tell you."

Apparently when bombs started falling on Valetta the family decided they needed an air raid shelter, expecting the bombing raids to extend beyond the docks and Grand Harbour into the centre of the Island. Originally there had been a small ante room leading from the hallway into our future dining room, the door to which had been closed and plastered over so that there was no indication of it in the hallway itself. On the dining room side the owners had fitted the door over the ante room creating a cupboard, and dug out a large cellar area which became their air raid shelter. He concluded "we believe they also dug a tunnel under the house and across the garden to the small stone house by the high wall. That was to be another way in because the big cupboard was to hide the door if the Germans came into the house to look for people."

The story took a long time in the telling, and we listened, open mouthed with astonishment, especially my mother who was already somewhat overcome by all her new experiences. Thankfully, at that moment, we remembered our manners and Charlie organised whisky and water for us all. As the details were explained again the conversation drifted into stories of the hardships the islanders had suffered during the War until, about an hour later, our neighbour rose. "Now I must return to my home. Do you know how to use the shelter Mr. Corke?"

"Use it? But there is no need to use it now - I hope!" he replied with a grin.

"Mushrooms, Mr. Corke, mushrooms! They grow very well down there. May I suggest you attempt to grow them, as we all enjoyed them when your compatriot grew them,and he sold them in the village."

Very intrigued Charlie fetched a ladder he had found at the back of the villa and, with a torch, went down into the cellar. The ground was slightly damp, but with a head-room of about six feet it would have been very useable as a shelter. The mushroom grower had left behind some free standing shelves, but despite closely examining the walls he found no trace of any other way either in or out, and we never discovered the tunnel under the garden to the little stone shed.

Charlie had no inclination to grow mushrooms - instead he had a ready-made dark room and took up photography, developing his own black and white films to send to the grandparents.

I took my mother to Dingli Cliffs which were rather frightening, Valetta which was awe-inspiring, Sliema which was disappointing, San Anton's Gardens which were cool and green and very surprising, the Silent City Mdina which was, as always, magical, to Mosta to see its magnificent dome - and then she ran out of steam.

"Jan, no more please. I've done and seen so much in three weeks I'll be glad to go home for a rest!" She spent her last two days slip stitching the loose covers, playing with Nic and finding room in her luggage for presents she had bought for everyone (it seemed) at home. As we waved her goodbye from the viewing balcony on her overnight flight back to the UK even Charlie shed a tear – he and his mother in law were always good friends.

As for the gardener, he came regularly three times a week each winter and spring, and also collected the fruit which, apparently, was payment for his labour but he never once acknowledged my existence.

Doris

The play was over and Nain had left. Our exciting villa seemed cavernous and overpowering, its cold tiled floors hard and unyielding, white dust covering every surface.

Getting to know Doris helped us all to feel more settled. She had a round, calm face, a beautiful smile and endless patience. The day after Nain departed she arrived with an enormous cloth of a rough sacking material, and announced she would wash the floors, and that this would be her first task each day. Disappearing to the back of the house she returned with a large metal bucket half filled with cold water and set off on her knees, working from one end of the house to the other.

"Doris you can't do that! Please, it's too much for you" I protested.

"Madam this is the work at all the houses. It is the best way to make the house cool and clean. It is no trouble to me" she insisted, and I realised I had a lot to learn.

She also expected to wash all our clothes by hand, in cold water in the old stone sink in the scullery. "We can't have that" Charlie announced and the following Saturday we went to Sliema and bought a clothes washer, which he installed in the cloakroom at the end of the hall. In Birkirkara clothes washing machines were still a novelty in 1963 and, for the first week after this magical machine arrived, Doris and Nic would stand together in silence, fascinated as they watched the clothes tumbling back and forth. Then, one day, it suddenly stopped, fully loaded. "Madam, madam, quick, quick, come!" she called as they both came running to find me. We all ran to the cloakroom only to find the clothes motionless, but fortunately with no sign of water leaking from the machine. My first thought was "Nic"!

"Doris, has Nic been fiddling with the knobs on the front?" I asked sternly.

"No, no, he has been by me !" she protested, loyal as ever to him, and I had to accept that for once he was not the culprit.

Back from work Charlie went up to the roof to inspect the tank. He was back in ten minutes. "It's not surprising it won't work!" he exclaimed. "The pipes leading from the tank into the house are clogged up with rust! There isn't enough water getting into the washing machine, so it stops automatically. The plumbers will have to sort it out."

On this occasion, a phone call to the agent did have a quick result. Next day five of them arrived. "Oh no, not those plumbers again" I muttered as they trooped in, smiling broadly, but this time they had at least brought their tools and a ladder.

"Madam, we must inspect the tank" said the older man as they set off up the stairs.

"But you inspected it just a few weeks ago" I protested. "You told me then that no work was needed."

"Madam, this is a very old house. Many times many things will go wrong very quickly" and they disappeared. Half an hour later they returned, announced that water was now flowing through the pipes to the machine and departed, the oldest man grinning happily, clutching a handful of English pound coins.

With his Nain gone Doris became Nic's new companion, and also his playmate in complicated games making long lines of cars under chairs and tables, or trailing round the house and garden searching for bits of flex or old wire which he entwined round his bike or door handles, or poked into hinges or any other convenient hole he could find. In the garden he dug the soil, filling his wheelbarrow to make "concrete" as Doris went back and forth, patiently filling and refilling his watering can. One afternoon an unexpected rain storm turned the holes he had dug into glorious, bubbly quagmires, and even Doris could not persuade him to stop covering himself in mud. He came running into the house, a big smile creasing the cake of mud coating his face as he yelled "look, concrete for a wall in the garden!"

Charlie was delighted at the signs of an engineer in his son - until drains caught Nic's attention. "Madam, the water will not go away in the kitchen." Doris came to find me, looking very troubled. "I do not understand why, but I am very sorry." After assuring her that it could not be her fault, Charlie was summoned to resolve the problem. He went outside and returned with his hands full of stones.

"Nic!" he groaned. "He has filled the drains by dropping stones through the grids! How on earth can I stop him doing that?"

We couldn't so enrolled him in a play school!

Another object of great interest to Doris and Nic was the sewing machine. The day after Nain's departure Charlie had come home with a large box. "Jan, I've got a surprise to cheer you up" he called.

"He is thoughtful" I said to myself as he opened the box with a flourish and a big smile, only to reveal an electric sewing machine.

"Why on earth have you bought that? I hate sewing! "I exclaimed.

He laughed and said "Cheer up, it's for me! I'm going to make the curtains!" I had forgotten that we bought extra material to match the suite in the lounge, and Doris and Nic stood together as Charlie sent the needle whirring up and down, 'hands free' and apparently by magic until they realised that he had a foot pedal hidden under the table! After a couple of evenings the curtains were ready and had been hung, and with a few cheap and cheerful pictures, and big vases full of colourful plastic flowers, the rather drab lounge was transformed.

The dining room was also a great success, but the walls were white, and despite having deep red curtains, with no heating it always seemed very cold. "I think we'll ask the landlord if we can paint the room pink" Charlie suggested a couple of weeks later. "It'll give us something to do."

Somewhat nonplussed by this unexpected interest in his client's property the agent happily gave us permission, but when we stood back to survey our handiwork the walls and the curtains appeared to be several shades darker than we had anticipated. "Can't live with that – it's too red and hot" was our joint verdict. Down came the red curtains and back went Charlie to the market in Valetta, returning with cotton in a beautiful dark olive green, again with a random pattern of flowers. Out came the sewing machine and we had curtains which were a perfect foil against the pink walls.

Early in December Next Door invited Nic to their little girl's birthday party. I was not specifically invited and could see no reason to stay with him, but when Doris went to collect him she returned looking very embarrassed. "Madam the children were not alone. The maids were there so they would not be naughty." Unaware of this local etiquette I was also embarrassed and, as they never invited him again, or asked us to go round, we assumed that either Nic had been very naughty or that our meat, fish and other perishables had outstayed their welcome in their freezer.

Nain's painting

OUR FRIEND FRED

We eventually realised that the Service personnel instinctively separated themselves from local people, and certainly never referred to local politics. However, as civilians we had no such constraints, and our friendship with Fred gave us a unique insight into the lives of the Maltese, as well as into their politics.

One evening early in 1964 we were at a rehearsal when a stranger wandered in from the street. He was short and stocky, balding with an oval face, beautiful teeth, very expressive hands one sporting a large, gold signet ring, and wore heavy black spectacles. With almost perfect English he was obviously well educated, but explained he nevertheless wished to improve his language skills. He asked if he could join because amateur dramatics would provide words he would not otherwise come across. This was Fred.

Always willing to help with building the scenery and organising the lighting, and spending many hours backstage, he soon realised that he and Charlie had left wing political views. "Come for a coffee" he suggested one evening in February 1964 "and I will show you the old Valetta."

I was very intrigued. Republic Street was closed to traffic when the cool of the evening allowed the citizens of Valetta to stroll along its length, women young and old in their latest fine dresses, the men in suit and tie, eyeing up the groups of girls as they laughed and chatted, pretending not to notice the potential suitors. "Is it very different to the usual Valetta?" I asked rather mischievously as Charlie, driving down a familiar route reminding him of his visit to the "mad Professor" a few weeks before said "I came here when I had impetigo to see an odd doctor who was recommended by the site foreman. He was in a tiny side street off Archbishop Street."

"Ah, so you were introduced to the Gut!" Fred chortled. "It's the one place where the Church can't stop men being drunk, or going to prostitutes. It's Strait Street, world famous, a great place!"

All doors were firmly shut as we wended our way down several alleyways in the dark, where mangy cats sat immobile on thresholds, and furtive figures, suddenly illuminated in the car headlights, created a sense of mystery and menace. A shaft of light suddenly appeared ahead as Fred said "please stop, and it will be safe to leave your car here."

As we sat in a noisy, shabby café, where he seemed to know everyone, Fred said "I come to this part of our capital often. I was not born here, but I come to remember that we have never been independent, always ruled by one of the big powerful countries. We must carry on fighting for it! Did you know that since the end of the War our party has been fighting the Catholic Church, and the British Government?"

"What is your party?" Charlie asked.

Fred leant across the plastic topped table, hands clasped, his eyes unexpectedly serious. Taking a deep breath, he said earnestly "the Malta Labour Party, the only party for these people here! That is why the Church has tried to destroy us. They try to control us with fear. If you vote for Labour you commit a mortal sin."

He paused. "You are not Catholic I assume, so you are

not aware of their power. You will not know how the priests will tell poor people that it's a sin to read the MLP newspaper. Last year the bishops sent letters to the priests telling them to tell everyone not to vote for the MLP, and they should ring the bells in the Church if someone from the Party was making a speech in the square. In the end they ordered the father confessors to refuse absolution if a person would not promise they would not vote for us!"

He stopped and leant back in his chair. "Now you see why we are still fighting! Dom Mintoff our leader went to Oxford University, and is a qualified civil engineer as well as an architect. When he came home he could see how the poor were kept under the foot of the Church, and now the British have joined with the Bishops against the people because we asked for independence." He leant back against his chair, and with a deep sigh said quietly "now we are fighting them both!"

Neither of us knew how to respond, and it all sounded rather far- fetched. Taking a sip from my Cisk I said, rather hesitantly, "Well, it all seems quiet now."

"Ah yes," he replied with a grimace "that is because Dom made a big row when the British sacked forty dock workers five years ago. Your Conservatives said we are still a colony and ruled us directly from London, and then made the Nationalist leader here the new prime minister without an election, and now we will have to wait for the next elections."

To change the subject I asked "What is the Maltese language exactly?"

He smiled "Exactly? That is a difficulty! It is a proper language, our national language. In the beginning it was a mixture of Latin and Arabic, and over many centuries Italian words from Sicily, and now more from English have been added in, so you see I cannot say exactly!" and he grinned.

He told us that he was a civil servant, a friend of Dom Mintoff, and a leading member of the MLP. He could never resist starting a debate about the Catholic Church and how it kept most people in a subservient position that could only be resolved by socialism. Unusually he was unmarried, and said he lived alone. "I have a small house and it is in a field near Marsaxlokk. It is many miles away from here, at the south end of the Island. You must come to visit me so we can swim and dive in Peter's Pool." He insisted that we left him at the bus terminus in Floriana, and we drove home in silence – he had given us much to think about.

"There is one good thing about the Church" he announced one day. "We have so many holidays for festa because we have so many saints! Now, next week I will take you to the races. It will be the 29th June which is the festa of St. Peter and St. Paul and there will be the l'imnarja in the Buskett Gardens."

This was a two day event, a festival of folklore, music and dancing, starting in the evening of the first day when families brought picnics and stalls produced huge quantities of fenkata, a rabbit stew, always accompanied by the local wine. "Do they make the stew there?" I asked Fred.

"Of course, of course! The rabbit must be very fresh so you can pick the one you want from the cages." No thank you I thought, and found an excuse not to go to the evening festivities, but we promised to go to the races. "When did the races first start?" I asked.

"With the Knights and are now a Maltese tradition" he explained. "The jockeys are all amateurs, and sometimes I think they want it to be like the chariot racing in Roman times and it can be quite dangerous! Before the last War horses came here from North Africa, but they all had to be slaughtered when the bombing started."

He explained that, after the feasting, the crowds spent

the night wandering round the various exhibits of local produce, especially the honey, watching the marching bands and traditional singing and guitar playing. Poems written by village poets became spontaneous songs, and the festivities continued until everyone went home at first light for a sleep.

On the second day we joined Fred for the races. There were no stands and the makeshift racecourse was lined with excited and cheering people of all ages. The horses and donkeys thundered past, dust and grit flying from under their hooves onto the onlookers as we all cheered and waved at the bareback riders gripping the reins, or clutching their steed round the neck. Eventually, the races were over, and all the proud winners were awarded with banners made of brocade which, by tradition, they would present to their village church to be used as an altar cloth.

Apart from the amateur dramatic society Fred had no part in our social life, always having a reason not to come to one of our parties, but he became a great friend often visiting or going to the beach with us. Until we left he remained a bit of a mystery, but on our return to the UK we continued to follow events in Malta, exchanging letters and Christmas cards.

The elections in early June 1971 resulted in a resounding victory for Mintoff, and coincidentally that was the year we drove to Malta for a holiday. We did not let him know we were on our way, and had no phone number for him. On our first Sunday we drove to Marsaxlokk early in the afternoon, through the silent village, all doors shut for the siesta. We found the narrow dusty lane leading to his house and trooped up to the familiar front door, lizards scuttling out of cracks in the walls of the field as Nic ran ahead calling "Fred, Fred we've come to see you!" We knocked but no-one answered for several minutes – then Fred in shorts and a singlet appeared.

"Charlie, Janet, come in, come in! Let me introduce you

to my cousin Joyce." He may have been unmarried but he was not alone.

After much hand shaking and hugging Fred asked "and who are these little ladies?", holding Charlotte and Emma's hands.

"You remember we had Charlotte when we were living here?" I replied "and Emma arrived three years after we went home."

"Of course, of course, all beautiful children! I had forgotten! Now Charlie my friend, we must have a swim in Peter's Pool, as we did many times. Come, we will all go!" Whilst the men dived and swam a stilted conversation between Joyce and myself was, thankfully, constantly interrupted by us both darting about the rocks to make sure the children didn't fall into the sea twenty feet below. Back at the house Cisk beer for the adults and lemonade and biscuits for the children appeared. Fred and Joyce were full of the Labour win at the election, explaining how Mintoff's policies would help develop the public sector and the welfare state, provide for gender equality in salaries, introduce civil marriage, decriminalise homosexuality and adultery, all with the interim objective of independence and the ultimate objective of Malta being declared a republic. Over many years the MLP pursued Mintoff's radical policies with some success, but not without several crises, violence and civil disobedience.

Immediately after the election, events moved very quickly. By the time we returned home from our six week trip Mintoff had annulled the defence agreement with Britain, expelled the Governor-General, sacked his own police chief, expelled all American and NATO Forces and formally requested Britain to remove all its forces by the 1st January 1972. In North Africa, wily Colonel Gadaffi soon observed the growing rift between the two countries, and lent millions of dollars to Malta to replace its lost income from Britain. In return Mintoff entered into a Friendship and Cooperation Treaty with Gadaffi, imposed Arabic as the official language for the two islands, opened the first mosque in Paola, and a Libyan Arab Cultural Institute in Valetta. He maintained his opposition to the European Union and finally established ties with North Korea and Roumania, but that was a step too far.

At the end of the War many Maltese men had emigrated to the UK and Australia looking for work, leaving wives and children behind. Connections with Europe and Great Britain remained strong and, in many cases, very personal. Hurtling towards the world's communist block proved too much for the Maltese people. After a huge row in the MLP Mintoff resigned as Prime Minister and leader of the Party in 1984, but remained a back bencher, maintaining his influence on events.

August 1988 found us back on the Island again, staying in a villa with some friends, and invited Fred to dinner. Apparently untouched by the years that had passed, he was his usual chatty and charming self, delighted to meet Emma, now a glamorous seventeen year old, and our ex-service personnel English friends, very curious to have our reactions to all the changes that had taken place since we had lived on the Island in the mid-sixties. A happy convivial evening passed with no reference to the Catholic Church or local politics.

On the 21st December 1988 Pan Am flight 103 was blown up over Lockerbie. Gradually the friendship between Dom Mintoff and Gadaffi, and the connections between Libya and Malta, appeared to point to a Maltese involvement with that terrible event, and doubts about the friends we had made, particularly Fred, inevitably crept into our minds.

In 2002 Nic, now with a his own family, visited Malta on holiday and went to the familiar address. Strangers were occupying the house, no-one knew anything about Fred, and he seemed to have disappeared without trace - always an enigma!

The famous Gut (Strait Street)

'NORMAL FRIENDS'

Other friends were not as exotic or mysterious as Fred. The amateur dramatic society was a great place for meeting people because everyone joined to have fun. We also discovered there were other, serious minded British civilians on the Island working at various commercial enterprises, but nobody else lived 'out in the sticks' (as David our naval friend called Birkirkara) like ourselves..

Most were in their thirties, except for one very dear couple in their early fifties, Dorothy and Alan. Quite elderly compared to the Island's normal age range, and with grown up children in the UK, we became very fond of them. Always incredibly welcoming there was just one snag – Alan was a great conversationalist. As a commercial traveller based in Malta his work took him to the Middle East and North Africa selling European style clothes to rich educated women who, even in the mid-twentieth century, wore them under their all - enveloping burkas. His wife never knew whether he was in Libya or Egypt, Algeria or Morocco, and he had many fascinating tales to tell on his return of incredible wealth on the one hand and dire poverty on the other. A military coup in Syria, a war between Morocco and Algeria in 1963 and the establishment of the Palestinian Liberation Movement in1964 were some of the events which made the area ever more unsafe, and he told us he never felt at ease in any of the countries he worked in.

Consequently, once back in safe territory, and having

been deprived of conversation in English for maybe two or three weeks, there was no stopping him, as we discovered when, one night, we arrived back home at two thirty.

With no clock in their flat a surreptitious glance at a watch was very tricky. "Can't go there again" groaned Charlie as he dragged himself out of bed at six the next morning. "We'll have to find a way to leave earlier!"

A few days later he came home with a new pair of long trousers. "I know I'll be too hot when we go to see Dorothy and Alan next time, but now I can put a tiny alarm clock in my pocket and it can buzz against my leg to tell us when it's time to go home!" Problem solved.

Many of the Service wives accompanied their husbands from one posting to the next but, more inclined to a less hectic lifestyle, Peggy had remained in the UK until David's posting to Malta had made it possible for them to go abroad with their three sons as a family. Not so much a 'Services wife' as many I met, she and I soon became great friends, and we spent many happy times on the beach with the two little Nicholas boys. A small bay called Bahar ic-Caghaq, with its countless rock pools and a narrow strip of fine limestone gravel leading into the shallow clear water, was perfect for the two boys, keeping them happy for as long as Peggy and I were prepared to sit on the rocks.

She introduced me to the Service wives who spent their days at the 'Club' playing tennis, swimming and socialising, always on the move, packing and unpacking, children in boarding schools in the UK, parents thousands of miles away. At the United Services Sports Club in Marsa the British, and many wealthy Maltese, enjoyed facilities harking back to colonial days. Ten acres of precious land had been commandeered by the British in 1902 to provide an 18 hole golf course, a full size polo pitch, a cricket pitch with practice nets, three squash courts and fifteen tennis courts (with showers next door), all surrounded by immaculate gardens. Obviously little thought had been given to the Island's chronic shortage of water when the Club had been established by the Victorians.

David and Charlie both loved sailing and entered a race organised by the Services. David borrowed a small, rather shabby yacht with faded sails from the Services Sailing Club, and the two men spent many evenings practising and getting used to handling the boat as a team. For David it was second nature, but whilst Charlie was far less experienced as a sailor he and a fellow engineer had, before we were married, built a small boat which we used to sail on Geirionydd Lake when we were living in Snowdonia.

The race would start in Grand Harbour, then the boats would sail out into open water, continue north-east towards Gozo, then around the small island of Comino and sail back down the east coast of Malta, finishing in St. Julians. When the big day arrived the two men viewed the other boats with dismay. "Stiff opposition! They've all got new boats, we won't stand a chance" exclaimed David, recognising several retired naval men as well as wealthy Maltese who were members at the Club. Whilst Charlie saw it as an exciting sport and a chance to have fun, David was very competitive and was immediately dejected about their prospects.

For May the wind was unusually strong and the sail northwards was exhilarating and effortless, but returning against the wind was a different story. Normally sailing in light winds many of the yachtsmen found it difficult to make headway and, when eventually within sight of the line of buoys indicating the finishing line, several of the boats got stuck off the coast opposite Sliema, some, unintentionally, heading back north. "This reminds me of sailing on a lake in Snowdonia, the wind all over the place!" exclaimed Charlie as he told David how we used to go sailing in the mountains with the wind constantly changing direction, the boat being buffeted about by the squally conditions. Making the most of this unexpected advantage Charlie tacked their way back and forth inching nearer and nearer to St. Julians, and to their, and everyone else's astonishment, they came second!

Over supper that evening Charlie exclaimed "I've had a great day, and I now know why David has seen so many seascapes!" After attending a naval school he had joined the Navy as a boy sailor and during a long and successful career in the Navy had travelled all over the world.

Another interesting couple were foster carers whose children attended the schools run by the Services. Kindly and welcoming, they were always prepared to help new arrivals like ourselves, but never allowed to forget a dinner they attended, along with various high ranking Service personnel and local politicians.

"I hate those posh dos" exclaimed Moira as she recounted the story for our benefit. "After all, I had three children to feed and organise before Maria arrived to baby sit, and we got to the Club just in time. When I found my place at this very formal dining table I was stuck next to this Admiral chap, all gold braid and medals, and of course I didn't know him. Anyway I'd had a stiff gin and tonic on the way in and managed to chat a bit whilst we were having soup, and he also loosened up a bit as the wine started going round, and I thought it might be ok after all."

She stopped for a moment, looked across to her husband and they both started laughing as she continued "then the worst bit happened! The main course arrived and by now I was chatting away, quite happy, and then everything went quiet and I saw that two couples sitting opposite to us, and the Admiral were all silent." Again she stopped.

"Go on, finish the story" said her husband, grinning at us.

"This is the best bit" he added unkindly.

"I looked down and saw why – I was cutting up the meat on the Admiral's plate and arranging the vegetables in small piles and away from the gravy – just as I do for the children!"

PARTY, PARTY, PARTY!

Part of Charlie's job involved dealing with representatives of companies, contractors and engineers who regularly flew in from the UK to deal with various problems. In the days before fax machines new plans or instructions had to be posted, but if there was an emergency, or a problem that required immediate attention, it was quicker for someone to fly out from the London headquarters with new drawings or calculations, rather than send them by post. Such a visit usually meant a party of some kind, or a dinner in the Phoenicia Hotel. My previous life in Snowdonia had been far removed from glamorous evening wear. "Charlie, I've got nothing to wear" I wailed.

"I'll ask Paul where his wife goes to shop "he replied, and several visits to a ladies' fashion shop in Sliema made a considerable, but necessary, dent in our savings.

The main contractor on the site was a well-known and respected Maltese firm, and in December 1963 it threw a Christmas party in the main hotel on the Island. Built in the nineteen thirties in the Art Deco style the Phoenicia Hotel was situated in Floriana, just outside the Kingsgate into Valetta. Severely damaged in 1942 during one of the German bombardments, it re-opened in 1948 with magnificent rooms, a terrace overlooking Marsamxett Harbour and (surprise, surprise!) sufficient electricity and water supplies to provide (amongst other things) showers in every suite, electric razors, ladies and gents hair salons, a private laundry and fabulous food in an enormous restaurant.

One little boy aged three

About two hundred guests included anyone of importance on the Island - politicians, church dignitaries and diplomats. With no expense spared long tables were loaded with savoury meals of meat, fish and poultry much of which, I discovered later, had been flown over from Italy. Elaborate cakes, fresh fruit, several refrigerated containers of variously flavoured ice creams and the traditional Maltese sweet of caramel flavoured nougat completed the meal, whilst the wine flowed unchecked. A trio played classical music in the background, and it was a fabulous evening.

Local etiquette meant that the men and women separated after the meal and I was cornered by a group of the wives. Although approaching middle age these women, with rich husbands, were still slim and glamourous, and because they never sun bathed had soft olive skin, and beautiful hands because they never had to work. They all knew each other and, talking in a mixture of Maltese and English, happily gossiped about the latest wedding, or a new baby, until one of them broke off. "Mrs. Corke I believe you are here as a civilian, not with the Navy as are so many of your compatriots. It would be most interesting to know how you find your life here. Which part of Sliema do you live in?"

"We live in Birkirkara."

"Birkirkara!" Pause. "Where is Birkirkara?"

"Just off Valley Road. We wanted a garden and managed to find an old villa." A long silence followed.

"Do you have a maid?"

"Yes" I replied. "She's a girl from the village and I don't know how I would manage without her."

"Only one?"

"Yes. It is plenty for me" Another pause.

"How many children do you have?"

"One, a little boy."

"Only one?"

"Er, yes. He's nearly three."

"Indeed!" and she turned away.

I was clearly an oddity. It was after midnight, and I was ready to go home when I heard uproarious laughter coming from the main ballroom. To my relief the group broke up, and I went to see what was going on. To my dismay our host and Charlie, dinner jackets tossed to one side, were both on their stomachs, stretched out on the ballroom floor.

"Oh no! He's drunk too much!" I exclaimed to the

Maltese lady next to me, thinking "he'll have disgraced the firm! We'll be on the next plane home!"

"No, no! This is a game that is often played in Malta" she laughed. "We have learnt it from the British navy, and it is a challenge that the men enjoy!" Our host had challenged Charlie to a bottle walking race. I had vaguely heard about these races, where two contestants held an empty beer bottle in each hand, stretched out on the floor and then 'walked' to the finishing line using the bottles instead of their hands.

Horrified, I watched as the manager of the hotel, with exaggerated precision, drew a line in chalk on the highly polished parquet floor. The other men had made a large circle and started taking bets, which was the cause of all the laughter. Four empty Cisk beer bottles were produced, the crowd pulled back and the manager shouted "Go!"

With my hand over my mouth I watched. Clearly our host had failed to take into account that Charlie was taller than his opponent and could stretch further towards the finishing line. It was a close run competition, and after both men had collapsed on the floor, puffing madly, they jumped up, slapped each other on the back, shook hands and returned to the bar. It was all over in less than a minute, but Charlie won by a hand's length.

"As you see, men enjoy these childish things!" my neighbour said kindly. I just smiled.

It had certainly been a memorable evening, but after a silent taxi trip home I exploded. "What on earth were you doing? D'you want to lose your job? I can't believe you could be so stupid!" I exclaimed.

Charlie burst out laughing. "C'mon Jan, we had a great evening! Men are the same everywhere – they enjoy stuff like that – it'll be fine!" And it was – thankfully!

One of the engineers was Maltese, again highly educated and with perfect English, but very different to our other highly educated friend, Fred. It soon became obvious that on the Island those who were rich were often very rich, and his family lived in one of the old, very beautiful houses in Valetta and had another house near Mellieha, to which they retreated in July and August to escape from the intense heat in Valetta.

The husband and Charlie became great friends and he and his wife were very hospitable, and often asked us to join them when they were entertaining friends in their Valetta home. Only wealthy, 'old family' Maltese could afford to live in a house in the centre of their capital city. The interior was immaculate with polished tiled floors, coloured marble set in to some walls, oil paintings hanging on others, exquisite porcelain ornaments, vases full of real, highly scented flowers and french furniture, spindly chairs, pale green, inlaid with gold paint, the seats covered in gold silk – and very uncomfortable.

I had no idea what to expect on our first visit but, remembering the lady in the house with the tuneless piano, I wore one of my smart new dresses, new high heel sandals, a string of artificial pearls and matching earrings and applied a touch of lipstick. Despite everyone's efforts there was always a slight awkwardness because, again, the men sat in one room and the women in another and I was often the only British woman present. The expensively dressed, middle aged lady next to me said "Tomorrow I am flying to Milan."

"Are you going on holiday?" I asked politely.

"Not at all, not at all. My daughter's baby is to be christened in one month's time. Of course, for such an occasion I will have a designer dress made for me, and I am going to the designer for - what do you call such an occasion......" and she paused.

"A fitting?" I suggested.

"Of course, of course, a fitting, and I always buy my shoes when I go to Milan." I felt distinctly underdressed.

A very different group were the ex-pats. Early in the summer of 1964, before I returned to the UK to have Charlotte (more later), we were invited by a couple we had only recently met to one of their legendary beach parties at Golden Bay. The husband had been in the Army, and retired to Malta because his pension went much further on the Island than in the UK.

Golden Bay is long and sandy. We joined a throng of tanned, well fed English people of varying ages but mostly retired, all with a general air of self – satisfaction. Our hosts had a trailer attached to their car which opened into a small bar with plastic glasses, a generous supply of alcohol and various snacks, a portable barbecue and coals, and trays of skewers some loaded with chunks of tuna or swordfish, others with chicken kebabs, whilst their friends had brought bowls of salad and fresh, crisp, flat loaves of the local bread. We were obviously in for a long evening.

A few of the guests were young enough to organise games such as handball and most joined in, their joints and muscles well- oiled by gin and tonics. I sat on a rock, kebab in one hand and a glass in the other, watching a group setting up a game of rounders. Talking very loudly they organised themselves into two teams, marking the four bases with various bits of clothing, arguing amongst themselves until one man shouted "Right, we're ready! I'll be the batter."

"Don't run too fast Sally, your new hip isn't up to it yet" he shouted, whereupon one of the women took fright, collapsed on to the sand and burst into tears. Taking no notice of her the game continued, getting noisier and more disorganised until the batter fell over and couldn't get up without several players pulling his arms to haul him on his feet, shouting and hooting with laughter.

I surveyed the group with dismay. In the soft light shed by the moon hanging over the bay, several large, Maltese families were scattered about the beach, having come to make the most of the cool air blowing off the sea. The ageing, lumpy figures silhouetted in the moonlight, leaping up and down, shouting to each other must surely have appeared ridiculous. Relieved that there was ample space for the local families away from my rumbustious middle-aged fellow-countrymen, a longing for the green, wet, Welsh hills rushed over me, and I was thankful that the darkness hid my sudden tears.

Lastly there was our 'fun' group, friends we had met as civilians and those in the Services. Constantly on the move, always making new friends and acquaintances, they were unfailingly hospitable and welcoming. On one occasion Peggy and David invited us to join them at a naval summer ball, and on a warm, still evening in June 1965 we were all sitting outside on a terrace at the Club, vying with each other as to who would be the first to spot 'Early Bird', a communications satellite which had been launched in May. A tiny bright speck of light, it would be clearly visible in the clean atmosphere above the Island, and everyone was excited, laying bets as to who would see it first.

"There it is, look over there" shouted one excitable young naval officer, pointing wildly into the sky as he fell off the terrace, twisted his ankle, and spent the rest of the evening complaining loudly because he could no longer dance! Happy days!

CHRISTMAS 1963

It was the beginning of December. The sun shone every day, and we still wore our summer clothes.

In mid-December we decided to book two Christmas Day phone calls to the UK. However when we were informed rather brusquely that the last slot had been booked in September, we realised we were complete amateurs in overseas living. As we booked the calls for Boxing Day instead "may I remind you" said the telephone person "that you must be ready to pick up the receiver immediately, otherwise you will miss your three minute slots. You must be prepared!" I realised I was dreading Christmas.

Letters came from Grandma full of her usual Christmas preparations which spurred me on to make plans of my own. "I'll make a Christmas cake" I announced, and went to Sliema to the supermarket which I knew stocked dried fruit. There I bumped into an older woman, one of the naval wives I had met at a recent party.

"What are you going to do with all that?" she asked, inspecting the packets of dried fruit and other ingredients in my shopping trolley. "A Christmas cake? But my dear!" she exclaimed "don't you know it'll be a waste of time? With the humidity you'll be lucky if the cake hasn't gone mouldy within a week!"

Somewhat deflated I returned home. "I'm determined to

try and make one, but I'll need a big cake tin, and a storage tin" I told Charlie.

"That's great" he replied. "D'you remember the day we moved in and I had to go to Sliema for a new wick for the fridge? That shop had lots of cooking and kitchen things. Trouble, is I can only vaguely remember where it is." Next day I went to Sliema and near the hotel where we had had our first "disaster" I spotted a small door in an otherwise blank wall with a metal plate above it saying 'Electrolux'. As with most shops in Malta there was no glass front window but, guessing this might be the place Charlie had found, I entered a huge warehouse crammed with cookers fridges and washing machines. The 'Times of Malta' carried regular articles about "Malta's new consumer boom", and here it was!

There was no-one about as I threaded my way through stack after stack of cardboard boxes, and was about to leave when a voice floated out from behind one of the piles. "Madam what is it you are needing?"

A young lad appeared smiling in welcome. "Madam, you wish for a fridge or a cooker?" he asked hopefully.

"Well, no. I am looking for a cake tin" I replied. Complete bafflement crossed his face. I thumbed my way through my phrase book, found the word 'cake' and, showing it to him, said "I need a metal box to cook it in."

He suddenly grinned. "Ah, yes we have this! I will show you him," and leading me to the back of the shop he pointed triumphantly to a shelf loaded with tins of every possible shape, size and colour, and I returned home with both a cake tin and a large purple tin. The baking day arrived and, sliding the cake into the oven, I prayed we did not have one of the frequent electricity cuts, but the supply held out and six hours later I removed it with a sigh of relief - but where to store it until the big day?

"The air- raid shelter!" exclaimed Charlie and descended into the depths below the house. Once the Christmas cake was safely stored in the cellar we decided to throw a party on Christmas Night because, despite all the parties for Service personnel, we had discovered that many of our friends would be just as homesick as ourselves on Christmas Day.

I had told my acquaintance that I was also going to make a Christmas pudding but, taking heed of her comments, decided not to bother, but Charlie was so disappointed that on Christmas Eve I changed my mind - which was just as well because it became our Christmas Dinner.

We had been at a party in November when a young naval wife, happily inebriated, threw out an invitation to all and sundry to have Christmas dinner in their flat in St. Julians. "Come at midday for drinks and we'll eat turkey and all the trimmings at three" she announced, "but don't bring the children. They'll cramp our style!"

"What about Nic?" I asked Charlie. "D'you think I could ask Doris if she would mind looking after him?"

"If he goes to her house he'll have much more fun than if we have him on his own for the day – you know what he's like!" he replied.

Tentatively I approached Doris. "Doris, would you mind looking after Nic for a couple of hours on Christmas Day?" I asked.

I need not have worried. Her face lit up, a big sweet smile giving her answer. "Can I take him to my house? My family will take very good care of him." Nic duly went with Doris, and we set off dressed in our summer clothes.

Charlie had been keen to go for a swim, but we decided not to as it seemed we were in for a fairly alcohol-laden day. By two o'clock we were all very merry and also hungry, but carried on with the crisps and nibbles. No dinner arrived at three, or at four, our hostess darting in and out of her kitchen as steam, smelling strongly of vegetables, drifted into the living room, but there was no sign of any other preparations. By half four several guests had drifted away whilst others were asleep. I wanted to leave but Charlie was engrossed in conversation with two men who were planning a sailing trip to North Africa and trying to persuade him to accompany them. At last, our hostess emerged from the kitchen and burst into tears.

"What on earth's the matter?" her husband shouted.

"There's no dinner" she sobbed. "No-one told me the turkey was frozen. The middle is full of its innards and they're still not thawed out!"

There was total silence until one of the men, slightly drunk, grabbed her round the waist and started laughing, all the while dancing round the room as he shouted "Never mind we'll all come back next year!" We never saw the unfortunate young navy wife again.

Back home we were very hungry, so after egg and chips and several helpings of Christmas pudding we went to collect Nic. Almost dark the air was hot and humid as we wandered through the alleyways trying to find the house where Doris and her family lived. As usual the older men and women were sitting outside their front doors on hard, upright plastic chairs, the men smoking and idly watching the world go by, the women knitting. They all smiled or waved as we passed until one small, elderly man took Charlie by the arm and, whispering "come, come", drew us into his house.

A statue of the Madonna, almost as tall as our host, stood in one corner of the sparsely furnished room surrounded by candles, some on the floor others in various containers, filling the room with a smoky luminescence. "Please, you will have a Christmas drink!" he insisted and, producing three tiny glasses, poured out small (fortunately) amounts of a dark liquid, put his to his lips and downed it in one gulp, nodding and smiling at us to do the same. An intense sweetness hit the back of my throat as I gasped and spluttered and then had a coughing fit, whilst Charlie smiled bravely, shook hands with the old gentleman, took me by the arm and led me out before I disgraced myself even further. We never discovered what we had drunk – Maltese home brew?

At last we found the correct alley and knocked on a dull brown, wooden door. Expecting to find a tiny house, instead we stepped into a cool courtyard softly lit by electric lamps hanging on the walls, while stone troughs and various ceramic pots filled several corners with luxuriant greenery. On the other side of the courtyard a door opened and a jumble of children of all ages tumbled out, Nic amongst them.

Doris's father came to greet us followed by his wife, smiling shyly, and again small glasses were produced, but this time accompanied by a familiar whisky bottle. Hard chairs followed, and we sat in a warm glow of friendship and alcohol, everyone reluctant to make the first move. Nic had had a wonderful day with Doris's large family always ready to play games, and we eventually managed to persuade him to come home, but only by telling him we were going to have a party in our house.

Originally we had asked a few friends to come round, but somehow word got out and the gathering grew and grew. The Christmas cake was perfect, with not a trace of mould on it, and because it was all gone before the end of the party I produced the rest of the Christmas pudding, which also disappeared. I abandoned my efforts to persuade Nic to go to bed and the party was still in full swing in the early hours, Nic asleep on the settee.

One of our guests was a meteorologist who worked at Luqa airport. After completing a night shift on Christmas Eve he had slept all day, and arrived as fresh as a daisy, ready to make up for the eating and drinking he had missed. By two in the morning most of the guests had left, but he embarked on a long story about working in the desert in the Middle East when a dust storm had blown up affecting his instruments as he tried to divert a plane to Luqa airport, which was clear of the wind and the sand. Rambling on, becoming ever more technical, he looked round for another drink and noticed that Charlie and I were the only ones left in the room. "Never mind, the plane didn't crash" he muttered, suddenly very embarrassed.

He stood up, and I followed him to open the big front door as he stumbled into the hallway, stepped outside, missed his footing, collapsed on the top of the steps and fell asleep where he lay. I stared at him, then giggling uncontrollably called to Charlie "You'd better come here - he's out for the count!" Despite my rather befuddled state I found the card our friendly taxi driver had given me and, fifteen minutes later, between Charlie, myself, and the taxi driver, we managed to get our guest down the steps, through the gate into the taxi, Charlie and the driver holding him under the arms whilst I held his feet.

"Very good party!" grinned the driver. "Where must I take him?" Charlie and I looked at one another – we had no idea.

"The Club!" we exclaimed simultaneously as Charlie pushed a ten shilling note into the taxi-man's hand and sent our visitor on his way to the only place we could think of where someone would take him in.

Grandpa and Grandma had sent us a tiny, but real, 'Christmas tree' by post and, leaving the party debris where it lay I got Nic into bed and then we sorted out his presents. Charlie had made a little wooden garage which we filled with plastic cars, piled all the presents sent at great expense by various relatives, around the tree, and fell into bed hoping that, having had such a busy day, Nic would sleep for longer. At half past six he was awake, and our 'Christmas Day' had begun.

Oh for a Christmas in Snowdonia!

The best part of the holiday was the opportunity it gave Charlie to play with Nic, who kept on shouting "Come on Charlie – do jobs!" First they fitted a letterbox to the front door then repaired the fountain, which had mysteriously stopped refilling the pond. After lunch, having missed a swim on Christmas Day, Charlie declared he needed to go somewhere near the sea. We drove towards Grand Harbour and continued south to St. Thomas' Bay. A small bay with a sandy beach, surrounded by traditional stone built houses, it was quiet and peaceful, and as we ambled along the beach paddling in the warm water, we could see high, towering cliffs rising straight up into the blue sky from the sea which, whilst majestic and awe inspiring, were also mildly threatening when our binoculars revealed crumbling edges which appeared about to crash into the cobalt blue water below.

We drove round the coast, inland past Marsa Creek and Charlie's workplace, and then back towards the sea for a stroll along the promenade at Sliema. The wind had strengthened and big rollers crashed against the promenade spraying us as we, the only spectators, stood savouring the freshness in the breeze, watching Nic's cheeks regain a Welsh mountain-air glow. When the grigalata was blowing in from the east in the winter months, the seascape of heaving water and long brown rollers, topped with foam crashing onto the rocks, was somewhere to make for by those of us who longed for a wet day and a howling gale.

I glanced at my watch. "Charlie, we must dash back" I called "or we'll miss our phone slots!" Back home we huddled round the table by the phone as the minutes ticked closer and closer to six o clock. Five past came and went, and I was close to tears when the bell rang so loudly I jumped and dropped the receiver. We could only afford a three minute call to each set of grandparents and, because everyone babbled at once, nothing was said or heard by anyone that made any sense except "Happy Christmas" - and I was more homesick than before!

In true British fashion, tradition was upheld on the Island by the Malta Choral Society when every January they performed the 'Messiah' in Valetta. Built in the mid-nineteenth century in the neo-classical style, the interior of St. Paul's Anglican Cathedral was severe, a beautiful tiled floor doing nothing to relieve the impression of cold austerity. Pillars supported a flat ceiling devoid of any decoration, whilst the harsh light from fluorescent tubes along the walls on either side, made the interior even more unwelcoming, However we enjoyed the performance and, driving home, decided not to make unkind comparisons with performances we had both heard at different times in the UK. The glorious music overcame any mishaps, and we returned to our villa comforted by the thought that our Maltese Christmas had not been so miserable after all.

INDEPENDENCE

Coincidentally, both Charlie and the Islands acquired their independence during the summer months of 1964.

Nic would be three in April 1964. I was unable to work, and we decided it was the ideal time to add to our family. When I told Doris that I was pregnant her face broke into a huge grin, and she just said "Oh, another Nicholas will be lovely." Our Maltese doctor confirmed that the baby was due in late August or early September and with no access to the maternity facilities that were available to the Services' personnel, and no idea what local services were like, we decided I would return to the UK, stay with my parents, and have the baby in North Wales.

"Don't like the idea of being here on my own for three months" Charlie exclaimed, much to my surprise.

"You'll have a great time. Everyone will ask you for meals, and you can go swimming with Bill after work, instead of having to come home" I said brightly.

"Oh, I don't know" he replied glumly. "I suppose I can see a bit of Fred at the weekends when he's not at work."

A few days later he came home with plywood, canvas and various tools he had borrowed from the site and stacked them in the front room, still somewhat euphemistically called "Nic's playroom." "I've got to make something" he announced "so I'm going to make a canoe whilst you're away. It might be useful at some stage." It satisfied his longing to make something until, two years later, realisation dawned that he would have to leave it behind – which led to our 'little house' project, more of which later.

Nic and I left at the beginning of July 1964. I dreaded the flight, but he couldn't get on the plane quick enough running across the apron towards the propeller until a flight attendant, seeing my very pronounced bump, chased after him and placed him firmly on the lowest stair.

His letters soon made it clear that Charlie was missing Nic. After pulling a picture of him out of the developing fluid in his photography room, he wrote "I was thrilled to see his lovely smiling face, just like magic." That's when I realised he wasn't enjoying his new found freedom.

After I left the temperature soared to ninety eight degrees and, even at night, never went lower than seventy degrees, with humidity to match. His shirt sticking to his shoulders like a wet rag Charlie would return to the villa in the midday break to change and he wrote "Mrs. Next Door is pregnant and feeling the heat ! I was in the playroom last night when Mr. Next Door arrived home and I heard her telling him "it's alright for you gadding about, but what about me? It takes me all my time to move - and you – what do you care, gadding off until now!"

The high ceilings and thick limestone walls of our old villa provided some comfort, but his hands stuck to the thin air-mail paper as he wrote to me, and sweat ran off the end of his nose as he tried to sleep. He took a folding bed onto the roof but the idea failed because the mattress became damp and the metal frame ran with dew. I was very relieved to be in Wales, in the summer rain.

Shortly before I left we heard reports of trouble brewing in the Post Office in the UK. Wildcat strikes and work to rule meant that mail boxes were overflowing, deliveries slowed to a trickle, banks and businesses organised their own messenger services and millions of letters piled up. A huge demonstration in Hyde Park, strikers wearing black suits instead of red, carrying banners saying 'Security from Tory Bandits' and singing as they were led by bagpipes and drummers through the London streets, had brought traffic to a standstill. We knew letters would take ages to arrive but wrote to each other every day, and more than one letter I sent, with 'Birkirkara' printed clearly on the envelope, ended up in 'Birkenhead' - before, eventually, being forwarded to Malta.

There were some lighter moments. Paul and his wife's social circle centred on the English community living in Sliema, mostly ex-pats and retirees, whereas our friends were younger Service families, and the two groups never intermixed. The Autumn amateur dramatics production was under way, and shortly after my departure the actors decided to practise their acting skills. The speaker on the phone in the site office was much louder than normal, making it impossible to have a private conversation - everything the caller said could be heard by everyone else.

On an agreed day the phone rang in the office and Paul answered. A husky, young female voice said "Charles dear, I'm so glad you're there. I need to speak to you." Knowing I was in the UK Paul handed the phone to Charlie, with no comment. Obviously in with the joke Charlie replied "Oh, right, right, I will speak to you later," and handed the phone back to Paul with no explanation. A few days later a woman with a strong Scottish accent rang. "Is young Charlie there? I need a quick word" she asked urgently. Again Paul gave the phone to Charlie who answered by making an arrangement to meet her, and Paul, giving Charlie a very quizzical look, took the phone back from him and, silently and very deliberately, placed it back on the cradle.

Much merriment ensued at the rehearsals as Charlie

recounted how Paul responded to the calls, and they decided to try once more to force him into enquiring what was going on. A week later another female voice, 'far back' and very loud, phoned.

"May I speak to Mr. Corke?" resounded round the office.

After a pause Charlie heard Paul say "Charles Corke? I regret he is out on site madam, and not available. I will tell him you called." Paul put the phone down, silently turned back to his drawing board, never asked for an explanation - and Charlie never gave him one!

Building the canoe kept him busy. He had covered the bottom in canvas when an RAF friend arrived with a large piece of a heavy, black and red, silky material under his arm. "Here you are Charlie, this will give you a top for the canoe" he said, dumping it on the floor.

Charlie had no idea what this obviously very expensive material could have been used for. "Well, that's very generous of you. Thanks, but what is it exactly?" he enquired.

"Come on Charlie, I thought you knew a bit about aircraft! It's an old sleeve target which we attach to a plane and tow it behind when we are doing anti-aircraft gunnery practice on Filflaletta! It's had a lot of rough treatment, but I thought you could cut it up and use it to cover the top of the canoe." Whether or not it had been acquired legitimately Charlie did not enquire, but set about cutting it to shape for the canoe, promising me to keep enough to make two cloaks as part of the costumes he was planning for Carnival the following February.

He went swimming every day and wrote "It's something to do to go along in the mask, which puts you in an isolated world of your own, where you fly (apparently) over mountains and gorges looking down into an alien world. I just cruise along about twenty yards from the edge and never touch the bottom for about half a mile and then come back. The sea was full of octopuses – or are they octopi? Anyway I tried to catch one but no luck. I put some lentils to simmer whilst I went swimming yesterday and then made croquettes and fried them following the recipe on the packet. I didn't think much of them so I treated myself to black currants and the top of the milk!"

Before we were married he cooked for himself when he was living in the cottage and (tongue in cheek) I suggested he rekindled his culinary skills by making his favourite meal – a casserole of steak and onions, assuming that such a meal in the heat was unlikely to stir his interest, but a few days later he reported he had made enough to last three days.

As the first combined power station cum seawater distillation plant that had ever been built, the work was challenging. Checking structural steelwork with the temperature at 100 degrees was bad enough, but when incorrect or unnecessary information arrived, or in the wrong sequence, confusion reigned and tempers frayed. Charlie's contract included holiday entitlement and he decided to go home for a few days, but en-route he had go to the firm's London office. He eventually arrived on the 31st July 1964 and returned on the 9th August convinced that, because all his cousins were boys, the baby would be another boy and we agreed to call him Benjamin, but 'he' turned out to be Charlotte!

On his return, he decided to reorganise the house, man-like never thinking I might object to the new arrangements. He mended a table in the lounge and replaced the old, useless mesh on the fly-screen in the bathroom. On top of a set of two drawers, he found a type of cupboard, separated them, nailed plywood across the top of the drawers, glued soft material onto the plywood and we had, as he described it, "........a base for the carry cot and ideal for keeping the sheets and nappies and bits and bobs all handy and tidy and out of the way."

He fixed new hinges on the doors of the cupboard, nailed

more plywood across the bottom, painted it white and stuck some transfers on it and put it in Nic's bedroom to keep his toys and books: I didn't tell him that expecting Nic to run up to his room every time he wanted a toy was completely unrealistic.

He reported he was rearranging our bedroom by pushing the two wardrobes together along one wall, leaving the chest of drawers on the remaining wall. Unfortunately, strong though he was, he had to remove all the clothes out of the wardrobes before he could move them, but did not like the new arrangement, and had to put everything back again.

He painted the little room downstairs at the back of the house, repaired the shutters, bought a second hand single bed and a chair and a pretty shade for the bare electric light bulb. Next day he asked Doris "Would you sleep here if we need more help sometimes?"

Her response was simple. "Can I can help with the baby?" she asked smiling broadly.

Charlie was only too delighted to reply "Of course!"

News arrived that my Morris Minor had broken down. The water pump had failed, but finding a replacement seal in a back street shop in Valetta he fixed it and I heaved a sigh of relief. Then I read " it's made me think of buying a new car.... we could sell your car, paying duty on it as if we had imported it, arrange to have it exported, and buy a new car free of duty. I have seen a Hillman I like and your car is at the end of its age ..... and it would be sensible not to have a convertible." It sounded to me like tax evasion and, legal or not, the reply he received swiftly ended that discussion.

Returning to the UK to have the baby meant I had missed the Independence Celebrations, but a letter arrived with the news that Charlie's oldest friend, Ken was arriving on the 23rd September 1964 for a few days, and I was delighted they could enjoy the event together, and have a short holiday. He wrote," Prince Philip is going to do the honours instead of the Queen. There'll be an aerobatic display over Grand Harbour, a Royal Navy Display again in Grand Harbour, and lots of fireworks. The Malta Government has concentrated on cleaning up the streets, organising a band march in Valetta, and the street decorations."

Later he wrote "The occasion has in general been quite a happy one.......the people more English than the English, with very decorous clapping........no dancing in the streets or noisy hilarity.......just a feeling morning would be here soon enough and better get to bed! Photographers for the TV and newsreels were going round the arena.....with cheer leaders to get the crowds to clap and wave to make action for their films! There were rumours that the MLP were going to make trouble ....but, apart from one of the foremen at the site, I've not met anyone who is whole heartedly for Independence. I went to the bar by the bus station in Birkirkara the other night talking to labour supporters.......and their attitude was voiced by one chap who said "it's alright for the MLP, but how can I be independent of Britain? All my life I've worked for the British, my father raised me on the wages from the dockyard, I was taught my trade by the British. I know and like them. If Britain was in trouble I couldn't stand by and do nothing. It wouldn't be right" and all the others were nodding their heads. Very surprising!"

However, I subsequently learnt that the decorous behaviour of the islanders was not matched by the behaviour of the British. Two relatively young men, both apparently unattached, had been of great interest to parents who had unmarried daughters visiting for the celebrations. A few years later Ken let it slip that he and Charlie had been invited to several parties which, whilst pleasant, were uneventful apart from one aboard a ship. It went on late into the night, and when the time came to leave, somewhat inebriated, they were both having difficulty navigating the gangplank back to the shore. Laughing and joking, and shouting their farewells, Charlie fell off the gangplank straight into Grand Harbour, leaving Ken clinging to the rope handles on either side.

"Man overboard!" some wag had shouted, whilst two equally unsteady guests, cheered on by the other revellers, threw lifebelts into the water. The loud splash in the black, filthy water fortunately alerted a man in a taxi boat, one of the sleek Phoenician-prowed djhaisas, always to be found in Grand Harbour, day and night. The lights from the ship revealed Charlie as he surfaced, spluttering and coughing but otherwise in one piece, being fished out by the taxi boatman - to great cheers from the other party goers still on deck. No wonder he kept that story to himself!

CHARLOTTE

A few days after Charlie returned to Malta the doctor told me everything was fine and, not anticipating any complications, I planned to stay with my parents for three weeks after the birth and fly back before the end of September. Charlotte was born on the 7th September 1964 but she lost more than a pound in weight after suffering trauma during her birth. In those days the medics decided that her crying was my fault, and I returned to my parents' house a week later with a very fretful baby where they were coping with Nic, who never sat still for five minutes.

Charlie had to be told about the unexpected problems and his letters became increasingly forlorn and anxious. I was desperate to return to Malta, but the doctor advised that I should wait for six weeks before flying back on my own with a crying baby and a hyperactive three year old.

Returning from Malta to Wales one large suitcase had been sufficient: going back with a baby was very different. With three suitcases and Charlotte in her carry cot, and accompanied by my parents, we travelled to London by train, stayed overnight in a hotel where the baby cried all night and all the following morning until, at last, on the 13th October 1964 we boarded the plane.

We were allocated four seats, two on either side of a small table, one each for me and Nic, whilst the hostess placed the carry cot across the other two, and as the engines roared into life for take-off, unbelievably, Charlotte fell asleep and slept all the way to Malta. I produced colouring pencils and books, but as soon as the Captain announced we could unfasten our seat belts Nic was off, up and down the aisle, chatting away to other passengers who were all, presumably, trying to settle down for the journey until he climbed into his seat and fell asleep.

As I was dozing off the plane suddenly lurched downwards. A loud shriek jerked me back to consciousness. "Maria, maria, ajjut, ajjut!" A middle aged woman on the other side of the aisle was clutching my arm, babbling in Maltese, crossing herself frantically, wailing uncontrollably and hanging on to me with an iron grip as the plane droned on. We bumped up and down as we crossed the Alps and still she clung on, crying and crossing herself, rivulets of mascara running down her face and under her chin onto a previously spotless white blouse until, at last, the air hostess came to my rescue. Miraculously neither Nic nor Charlotte woke up, but my fellow passenger's terror had communicated itself to me and my chance of a nap disappeared.

We arrived at Luqa in the early evening and I immediately saw Charlie standing at the exit gate, smiling broadly. I was so relieved that I ran forward holding Nic tightly by the hand, but he - having none of it - was so delighted to see his father that he pulled free and jumped into Charlie's arms – which was when I realised that the carry cot had vanished. "Jan, where's the baby?" Charlie asked urgently.

For a second I was so exhausted I just stood there, speechless, but then panic set in. "Quick, quick, we must find someone who can help! Hang on to Nic" and I ran off, pushing past anyone in my path, desperately wondering where to find someone in officialdom to raise the alarm - but there was no need. Above the noisy, milling throng I caught sight of the carry cot, apparently floating above and over the heads of the crowd.

I shouted to Charlie "Quick, look - your daughter's over there! Go and fetch her! Give Nic to me!"

He set off elbowing his way through the crowds, chasing after the cot until, catching up with a burly smiling Maltese porter who was carrying the cot on his head, Charlie grabbed his arm exclaiming "Hey that baby's mine!"

As I joined them I gasped "That's my baby! Where was she? Why have you got her?"

"Calm down Jan, let him explain!" protested Charlie as we saw the porter looking anxiously at a Maltese official in uniform who was striding towards us.

"Sir, Madam, there is a problem? I will ask this man for an explanation." After a long conversation in Maltese, accompanied by much arm waving, the official turned to us and explained that the porter had noticed the air hostess leaving the carry cot near a pillar, and seeing the baby inside he had picked it up, and was on his way to the Left Luggage Office. The official asked us "You are happy with his reason? If you are not I will arrest this man for you."

"No, no, not at all, we are very satisfied with his reason" replied Charlie, grinning happily. The official left, and our rescuer, refusing Charlie's offer of a generous tip, went off laughing and shouting to a group of passengers who, open mouthed, had watched this odd event whilst waiting for their luggage to arrive.

At last we were back home and Charlotte was still asleep. Charlie started to put Nic to bed as I unzipped the large suitcase to get some clean nappies – and stared at the contents. A layer of tissue - paper almost covered a silky fur coat glistening in the electric light. Carefully I lifted the paper a couple of inches and peered underneath.

"Charlie" I called "you better come here and have a look! I'm so tired I think I'm going a bit odd," and I started laughing.

He came across and also stared at the coat. "Why on

earth have you brought that back with you?"

"It's not mine Charlie! " Suddenly it was serious. "Perhaps we've got caught up with some kind of smuggling. We better look at what's underneath it." Feeling very guilty at prying at someone else's clothes and personal belongings we carefully removed the coat, revealing several expensive dresses and glamorous underwear, but then we stopped.

"There must have been two identical suitcases. What's on the label?" As a quick look confirmed the mistake, Charlie burst out laughing. "They must have had a nasty shock finding nappies and baby clothes when they unpacked! I'll ring the airport and tell them. Come on, Nic's in bed and Charlotte's quiet, so let's have something to eat, just us."

It was a lovely idea and Charlie had made a delicious meal for our return. "Oh Charlie, I can't tell you how glad I am to be back! I'll just settle the baby. What d'you think of her?"

He looked into the carry cot. "Well, I suppose she looks like any other baby, but she's a bit spotty. Is she OK?"

"Wait until she opens her eyes –she's gorgeous" I replied indignantly. Sitting on the bed I gave her a bottle, made her comfortable, keeled over sideways on the bed and was dead to the world until next morning, whilst Charlie spent the evening eating his meal alone, and whether the baby cried or not during the night I never knew.

Next morning, very early, Charlie dashed back to the Airport where he found an equally puzzled, rather elderly, man standing by the reception desk with our suitcase at his side.

"As you might have guessed, my wife and I are well past having babies!" he exclaimed.

"Yes, we had rather guessed that!" Charlie replied wrily. Smiling broadly, both men shook hands and departed.

The next few weeks were very difficult. Nic didn't want to go back to his little school, and it was a daily battle to get him into the car and, but for faithful Doris, I would have despaired. Charlotte continued to cry night after night as I wheeled her in her pram round and round the lounge, her cries echoing through the villa, whilst I went through two large bottles of vodka (neat) which I kept in the fridge.

Fashion girl

About a fortnight after I returned my dear friend Peggy came round unexpectedly and found me, thin, exhausted and looking a mess. As the mother of three boys she took one look at me and said "You need some help!" I knew I did, but as a civilian wife I had no access to the Services' facilities. That did not deter Peggy. As the wife of a naval officer she had access to people at the Military Hospital and that evening the phone rang. A very crisp business-like English voice said "Mrs. Corke? I understand you are having problems settling a new baby. May I suggest you add half a teaspoonful of sugar to her bottle goodbye" and the phone clicked off. I never had an opportunity to thank her but when I made up the next bottle in went the sugar. The result was miraculous. That night Charlotte slept for eight hours and at last my precious, sad little daughter started to put on weight and life began to settle down.

With blonde, curly hair and blue eyes Charlotte was something of a novelty, and Doris would put her in her pram and wheel her off to one of her numerous relatives in Birkirkara, carefully guarding her from over enthusiastic aunts who wanted to pick her up.

I knew that when they were with her both children were absolutely safe and would come to no harm.

One day Nic ran away. Fortunately Charlotte was in her cot, and I asked Doris to run towards the village, whilst I ran towards the main road. Everyone knew us and as an elderly woman came plodding up the alley towards me I just said "Nic?" and threw my arms up in the air. She grinned and replied "Iva, Iva" and pointed at a faded brown door in an otherwise blank wall on the other side of the road.

Tentatively I knocked and waited. No-one came to the door but after I knocked again a thin, hollow-eyed young woman opened it. I stepped down into a dark room lit only by a small window at the back, and a gentle glow from an offertory candle in a small dish, its light flickering over a small Madonna attached to one wall. As my eyes adjusted to the gloom I could make out a wooden table, two upright chairs, a bed and a chest of drawers, and in the bottom drawer of the chest lay a tiny baby fast asleep. The girl looked at me and said "Iva?"

Anxious not to wake the baby I whispered "Nic?" She smiled and shook her head, and I left, just as Doris and Nic came running down the road. She had found him playing with some of the bigger boys by the Church and, smiling shyly, said "I knew I would find him!"

A few days later I made up a parcel of baby clothes that Charlotte had outgrown, and knocked at the faded brown door but there was no reply. I asked Doris if she knew who the young woman was, but she was so evasive, and obviously uncomfortable, that I stopped my questioning. Some weeks later I had to phone the agent about another leaking tap and, after the usual pleasantries, asked him "Do you know what happened to the girl with the baby in the little room across the road?" After a long silence he told me she had had an illegitimate child, been turned out of her home and had nowhere else to live - as far as the rest of the village was concerned, she had just disappeared. Woe betide any girl who strayed.

MOVING ON - OR NOT?

I soon noticed that Charlie, despite the sleepless nights, was very cheerful, whistling tunelessly and giving me little hugs. I knew he was very relieved that we were all back together as a family and one evening, when he had been able to escape from the amateur dramatics, he said "That's the last time we are going to be living apart for weeks on end! We did enough of that before we were married."

"I know" I agreed, "but have you got something else you want to talk about?"

"Well, yes." A long pause followed, and I could see he was considering very carefully how to continue.

"Well, erm" he paused, and there was another long silence. He lit a cigarette, and started again. "When Ken decided to come out for the Independence Celebrations we chatted on the phone about his flights, and then he started talking about the alterations to their house in Grassendale Park."

"Yes?" Another silence.

Eventually he continued. "He told me about another house, up the road from his place which is for sale."

I stared at him. Chatting on the phone? Hoping Ken had phoned Charlie rather than the other way round due to the expense, I waited. An old house sounded ominous, and I hoped it meant no more than a bit of gossip from home. There was another long pause.

"Well, is that it?" I asked.

"Not really. It's a Victorian house, split into three flats. D'you remember it, a horrible brownish grey colour? It's at the top of their road, and looks down towards the river."

I had Charlotte on my knee, trying to persuade her to break wind, which I knew was lurking, and I was not very interested. "No I can't. Anyway, what about it?"

"Well, the flats are occupied, and the owner wants to sell but, although it's been on the market for years, the house is in such a bad state no-one has bought it. Ken brought the details with him." He could contain himself no longer.

Out of his briefcase came the Sales Particulars and several photographs. The agents had, as they always do, presented the house in a favourable light, but had admitted to Ken that the rendering had last been painted in 1933, and the interior had been badly neglected.

I listened in silence, still waiting for Charlotte to produce a half decent burp, as he gave me a detailed account of the house. I was dumbfounded. "Charlie" I said at last, "we are here for another year, maybe longer the way the job is dragging on, so why are you even thinking about a house in Liverpool?"

It had obviously been a light bulb moment for him and he simply said "I just know it's for us and we should get in touch with the agents."

"Really? Well, I can't see the point" I replied.

With the new baby taking up most of my time and energy I left him to it. He contacted the agents, told them we were interested and, having several architects as friends, found a chartered surveyor who, we were assured, could be trusted to give us an honest opinion. He was given instructions to provide a full structural report and we waited as letters between Charlie and Ken went back and forth, firing up Charlie's enthusiasm to ever greater heights until, about a month later, the surveyor's report arrived, with no detail spared.

Rot, wet and dry, had thrived in the wooden floors, the cellar had never been tanked resulting in rising damp throughout the ground floor, the rendering needed urgent attention, the original wooden windows were down to bare wood, the interior needed "total refurbishment"– and so it went on. At the end of three pages of dire warnings the surveyor concluded that "taking account of the subsidence at the side of the building the estimated value of the property is £1700.00, less the cost of demolition."

The average price of a house in the UK in the nineteen-sixties was about three and a half thousand pounds, and at last my legal training surfaced. "Well, that's that! " I pronounced. "Now we know why no-one will buy it! No bank or building society will take it as security for a loan, and it would have to be knocked down. We'd be left with a building plot, no money and nowhere to live!"

Despite his best efforts, taking me out for dinner, producing plans and details of what he would be able to do with the house, he could not fault my financial argument. We informed the agents that we would not be returning to the UK until the summer of 1965, and I assumed that meanwhile Charlie would go off the idea, or the house would be sold.

Christmas 1964 was happy and busy with the two children to plan for, and a proper turkey Christmas dinner at home. Due to return to the UK in August 1965, our Christmas cards informed family and friends that if they wished to visit the next six months would be their final opportunity.

During our phone call home on Christmas Day, we suggested to Charlie's parents that they come on holiday. They were nearly seventy years old, had never flown and at first they refused, but after much persuasion, and to our delight, they decided to come for two months. "Bring your summer clothes" we said. "February and March are late Spring here, so when you arrive you won't need woollies or coats or macs." Fortunately they ignored our advice. To our dismay their holiday coincided with the two wettest and coldest Spring months ever recorded on the Island, so woollies and coats were in use almost every day.

Shortly after they left a letter arrived from my mother. "Before you come home your brother would like to come for a holiday, and bring his girlfriend. Have you got enough room?" being obvious shorthand for separate bedrooms. I reminded her that she had slept in the spare bedroom, and that the other room on the top floor could only be accessed through our bedroom.

"Will that be separate enough?" I replied. I had met his girlfriend but, being 1965, her parents wanted to be sure they would be properly chaperoned before agreeing to her going abroad with her boyfriend. We assured everyone that she would have the use of the spare bedroom (no mice), and he would sleep in the tiny bedroom on the top floor.

Charlie was thirteen years older than my brother, and highly amused, as both my brother and his girl-friend were in their mid- twenties. We agreed to "keep an eye on them" - and ignored him as and when he crept through our room late at night. Nic was thrilled to see his uncle, and we all had a great time, but were somewhat surprised when before they left he announced that moonlight and the murmur of the waves as they sat on the terrace of a hotel in Sliema had overcome him, and he had proposed and been accepted. They returned home – and eventually both married someone else!

Other family members and a girl friend of mine all came for holidays during May and June, and then early in July 1965, about six weeks before the end of our original two year contract, everything changed. Charlie came home and announced that the firm needed him to stay in Malta for a third year because the scheme had hit unforeseen problems. "Why do they always leave it until the last minute to tell you these things?" I exclaimed. We were sitting in the garden after our evening meal, enjoying a glass of wine.

"Well, after this job is finished I learnt today that we'll have to go to London for a year, and then on to Hong Kong for three years." The village had gone to bed, the villa was dark and silent, and the idea of another twelve months in the Mediterranean sun with the scent of orange blossom filling the garden under the black, velvety sky was a very attractive

"So, what do we do?" he asked.

"About what?"

"The house. Did you think I'd forgotten about it?"

"Oh no, we're not going through all that again!" I protested. The shadowy, hot July evening was so far removed from dilapidated old houses in Liverpool that to make a momentous decision to buy a house was ludicrous.

He didn't reply, but drained his glass, then continued. "There is another possibility I suppose. I'm wondering whether to leave the firm. If I decide to do that then we could buy the house and return to Liverpool. I know I'd have no job, but I'll set up my own consultancy – according to Ken there's a lot going on in the country because of Harold Wilson's 'white heat of technology' plan, and I know lots of architects." A pause followed then he said "Ken rang me the other day and said it's still on the market."

"So you know the house hasn't been sold?" I asked, playing for time, although I had guessed he'd been talking to Ken again.

He smiled rather sheepishly. "Yes" he replied. Obviously he had already given that option serious thought, and now I would have to do the same.

"I suppose the firm will want a decision by tomorrow" I said rather sarcastically, as I tried to concentrate on all the implications. We had met several older couples, ex- service people, who had retired to Malta and become confirmed ex-pats. They rarely returned to the UK because "it's so cold and I don't have any warm clothes" as one lady explained. Their children were scattered all over the world, they produced photographs of grandchildren they had never seen, and I sometimes wondered how they would survive when one was left alone. The possibility of going to Hong Kong was exciting, but continuing our itinerant life style on engineering projects filled me with foreboding. Our children would end up in boarding schools in the UK, we would have no settled home anywhere, and the children would never know their grandparents. For hours we sat considering every possible outcome but one thing was clear - three years living in another British colony and we would become ex-pats too.

"It's such a huge decision, but returning to the UK means I could work - at last!" I said.

"Well, we can opt to stay here for the next year and save more money and then I could resign. Are you sure you'll want to work after such a lazy life out here for three years?" Charlie asked, so seriously that I burst out laughing.

"Of course! I didn't spend five years as an articled clerk to qualify as a solicitor without wanting to work afterwards. It'll be exciting" I replied. I never considered that I might not be able to get a job because unemployment in the UK was low. Charlotte would be two and child care problems never occurred to me. The Beatles were all the rage and life back home was suddenly an attractive possibility.

"So, we'll stay the third year and then go back to an old wreck of a house, and no job – are you sure?"

"Yes, after all I remember the Park has lots of lovely trees, and it's so near the river."

Grassendale Park overlooked the River Mersey. Built by the Victorians, most houses were abandoned by their owners at the outbreak of the Second World War as they fled to North Wales or the Lake District, leaving their homes to be requisitioned or taken over by squatters. In 1945 the Park was in a sorry state, but by the mid-sixties most houses had been retrieved by their owners, or sold for a song and restored. The house Ken was so interested in was the one remaining semi-ruin.

We bought the house in 1965 paying £1700.00 and against our solicitor's "strong advice not to proceed." We became landlords of a property we had never seen, occupied by tenants we had never met and hoped nothing catastrophic would happen until we returned, comforting ourselves with the thought of having some money in the bank from the rents of the three flats. However, two of the three tenants left, and we returned with less than half of the expected amount in the bank - and the "slight evidence of subsidence" in the surveyor's report turned out to be a big hole at the side where the mains drain had collapsed. Home sweet home.

FESTA 1965

The festa to honour St. Helen was celebrated in Birkirkara on the 18th of August each year, but going to the UK to have Charlotte I had missed it in 1964.

Grasping at any opportunity to have something else to think about, rather than our fateful decisions about the future, I decided to make the most of our festa in 1965. Doris, who would have the day off, was delighted to tell me how all the villagers participated in the event, preparations starting months in advance with door to door collections to raise money to decorate the Church, and to provide the usual spectacular firework display to end the festivities.

The evening before the festa promptly at six thirty, the event was announced by a fusillade of loud bangs lasting about five minutes, followed by intermittent bangs throughout the evening, culminating at half past ten with a rain of fire! Leaving Charlie to baby sit I went to the Square, where I recognised many of my neighbours amongst the crowds. St. Helen's Basilica, festooned with twinkling electric light-bulbs, was a magnificent spectacle. The doors and windows, grimacing gargoyles and other intricate carvings on the front of the vast building were hung with hundreds of different coloured lights, casting multi coloured shafts of red, gold, green and blue over and among the throng, all chattering excitedly, laughing and gesticulating towards the Church. The village brass band, all fifty pieces, was parading through the narrow streets accompanied by a gaggle of little boys, the noise echoing off the walls of the alleyways, and after covering my shoulders and arms with a black lace shawl I ventured inside the basilica.

Countless candles illuminated the smoky interior, heavy with the aroma of incense. The large wooden statue of St. Helen, resplendent in blue, red and gold paint, had been brought out of its glass case and placed in the nave to await votive offerings from the congregation, many on their knees in front of the statue, hands clasped, or fingering gold crosses hanging round their necks. Exquisitely embroidered linen cloths were draped over the altar, overlaid with green carob leaves arranged in intricate patterns and intermixed with religious icons. When I could drag my eyes from this glorious display I could see that the walls were hung with red damask from just below the ornate painted dome, high above, disappearing into the incense perfumed darkness. Priests in black habits, small men with a distinct air of self- importance, passed hither and thither before the altar, whilst nuns scurried about, dusting and re-arranging the already tidy and immaculate offerings. I found an empty chair and, as I sat taking in this extraordinary (to me) scene, a murmuring filled the space with a sense of excitement intermixed with a religious fervour so strong that I left before I, too, was overcome with emotion.

Back home I found Charlie sitting in the lounge listening to a concert on the BBC World Service. "Well, what's it like out there?" he asked.

"Pretty amazing! Charlie, can you be late for work tomorrow? I want to see the procession coming out of the Church."

"Thinking of converting?" He grinned.

"No of course not, but it's just so dramatic!"

At seven thirty next morning I found a place in the Square amongst a crowd of villagers awaiting the start of the day's events. The elderly had placed hard metal or wooden chairs by their doors, or on the pavement, waiting to see the statue pass by. Grandmothers, grey hair scraped back into a bun, their sunburnt, calloused hands covered in gold rings in celebration of the festa, clutched babies as they bounced and jiggled them on their knees. Bunting was slung from window to window as well as along the streets themselves, whilst those fortunate enough to have a house overlooking the street hung over their balconies, clutching coloured paper flowers to throw onto the statue as it passed.

The men were almost unrecognisable in blue or grey tailored suits, some sporting silk cravats and smart hats, shiny polished shoes completing their transformation. The women young and old, wore fine dresses, black lace shawls covering their heads, multiple gold necklaces and crosses hanging round their necks. No respectable woman in Malta left her shoulders or the tops of her arms uncovered at a festa, but gold bangles adorned their arms, some as far as their elbows, whilst earrings glinted as the sun caught the precious metal in its rays. Small boys in spotless white shirts, but as likely as not to be shoeless, darted between the crowds, whilst the little girls, in beautiful flouncy dresses embroidered with fine lace, walked demurely by their mothers, their small ears already adorned by tiny gold earrings.

The heat was building up as I made my way towards the front, the few small patches of shade already taken by old ladies, heads covered, hands clasped as a fervent intake of breath rose from the crowd. At precisely eight o' clock the mighty bell rang out, its chime vibrating across the mass of spectators as St. Helen emerged from the Church swaying perilously from side to side, carried high on the men's shoulders, whilst others carried banners depicting saints, angels, crosses and other religious images as they walked on either side of the statue. Led by the priests and other church dignitaries the huge procession started its long pilgrimage, winding its slow solemn way through the main streets, followed by anyone who could walk, all accompanied by an out of tune but very loud brass band.

I ran back to the house so that Charlie could go to work and a couple of hours later, with Charlotte in her pram and Nic attached to it with a piece of strong tape, I returned to the Square, and finding a small space under an oleander tree I waited to see the procession's return. With their last faltering steps, sweat running down their faces the men, exhausted after three hours in the heat, took their heavy load up the steps into the coolness of the Church, the massive wooden doors swung shut and a mighty cannonade crashed around us.

Duty done, the rest of the day was for music, dancing, singing, food and wine. Special food had been prepared, houses guarding their age-old different recipes using rabbit and various herbs for a special festa meal. The local wine replaced the familiar Cisk beer, whilst everyone spent the afternoon watching races and other activities in the Square and the wider streets until late into the evening when, after a last furious burst of cannonades and brilliant fireworks exploding over and over again into the night sky, peace at last descended on the village and we were able to settle the children to sleep and go to bed.

"How would you compare the festa to a cymanfa ganu in Llanrwst?" Charlie asked me.

"I couldn't!" I replied.

A BOMBSHELL

At the end of August 1965 we sat in the officers' mess at the airport with some friends, both of us with a stiff whisky, watching the regular BEA flight disappear into the evening sky, taking with it the signed documents that would complete the purchase of the house.

"I really don't know what my parents will make of it, but it's too late to back out now" I said. "What about your Mum and Dad?"

"No idea" Charlie replied. "I told Ken not to say anything to them until we have explained what we've done" and he smiled, rather uncertainly. Our friends clearly thought we had made a terrible mistake, and by the time we had finished our drinks we thought we had too.

"I've never met anyone who is going home to a house they've never even seen" exclaimed one of the wives. "You must be mad!"

We drove back home in silence, and when we returned to the house Charlie stopped suddenly in the hall opposite the door to his workroom. "All this talk about going home has made me think about my canoe. What am I going to do with it?" We looked at one another- there was no answer. We had told everyone at home that we would be staying in Malta for another twelve months, but courage to mention our future plans had failed us each time one of us had written a letter to our respective parents. However, events overtook us.

Next day a letter arrived from my mother. "We're dying to see Charlotte, and as it's her first birthday next month we're coming for a visit." Early in September 1965 my mother returned, this time accompanied by my father. Not seeing the grandchildren for a further twelve months had given her an excuse to come for another holiday, even persuading my father who was even more terrified of flying than I was, to accompany her.

They stayed until the end of September, but we decided to wait until their last evening before dropping our bombshell. "We don't want to spoil their holiday" I said, making feeble excuses, because, in reality, I was very apprehensive.

"Well, they've got to know sometime" Charlie replied and, ever the optimist, booked a meal at the only up-market fish restaurant in Sliema. The meal was delicious and Charlie bought a bottle of French wine, which we knew my father would appreciate, rather than the local brew at half the price. We sat back, replete, and as my father slid the paper off the end of his cigar I kicked Charlie under the table, our pre-arranged signal.

"We have some news for you before you go home" he started. "No point in writing when you are here with us."

"Another addition to the family?" my mother asked hopefully. "Three would be nice – I always wanted twins myself" she added inconsequentially.

I had not expected this response. "Oh, hold on Mum, Charlotte is only twelve months old" I protested "and anyway, two is plenty. Shall we get another bottle of wine?" and gave Charlie another kick.

"Yes, let's do that!" she replied. "After all, we won't see you for nearly a year" and she smiled fondly at us.

Another ten minutes of chit-chat passed, but when our glasses had been replenished the dreaded moment was upon us.

Taking a deep breath Charlie announced "We are coming back to the UK when this job finishes next August, not to London but to Liverpool. I've decided to resign from the firm, and we've bought a house."

The house we'd never seen

My mother stared at me in disbelief, whilst my father took a hefty swig from his wine glass. There was no response from either of them until, after a long pause "Have you a job to go to?" he asked, puffing frantically on his cigar.

"No, but I am going to set up my own consultancy firm and Jan is going to get a job. The house we have bought is tenanted, but there will be enough space for us to live there as well." What a fibber, I thought!

We spent the rest of the evening trying to make the whole plan sound feasible and sensible. Knowing we were not going across the world to Hong Kong would, we hoped, persuade them that everything would work out, despite the uncertainty that was inherent in our arrangements. "How on earth could you buy a house without seeing it? What is it really like? Even if there is enough room for you and the children, as well as all these tenants, it may not be suitable" my father said disapprovingly. "Just as well we have enough room for you to stay with us when you get back whilst you sort yourselves out" he concluded, looking at my mother.

My mother glared at me. "How d'you know you'll be able to get a job?" she asked. "You won't have worked for years by the time you get back."

She was right. "Oh, it'll be fine" I replied airily, although I knew nothing about the job situation for solicitors in the UK. "Solicitors are always needed. There's bound to be something in a big city like Liverpool" I concluded dismissively.

"I hope you're right" she said ominously.

As my mother and I squeezed into the back of my car she exclaimed "Oh Jan, you two are terrible risk takers! Where on earth d'you get it from?"

An early night was required as they were leaving next morning, and thankfully there was no time for further discussion. They were very subdued as I drove them to the airport, my father because of his fear of flying, my mother because she hated leaving the grandchildren. "We'll soon be back, it's only ten months until the end of the contract" I said, trying to lighten the mood.

"Provided it isn't extended again" she replied gloomily. "Please don't make any more dramatic decisions" she added shakily as she gave me a final hug. "Your poor father is unhappy enough as it is!"

As soon as he came home I told Charlie "You'd better let your parents know in case they ring my mother to ask about their holiday."

"Oh lord! That would be a disaster! I'll phone them now"

he replied as I went upstairs with Charlotte. "Hopefully they can't be too mad at me in three minutes!"

"Well" I asked later, "how did it go?"

"Dad answered, and when I told him he just said 'Oh, here's your mother', and Mum just kept asking questions and not waiting for my answers! I'll have to write to them, but at least they know!"

THE LITTLE HOUSE

Decisions having been made we settled back into our usual routine, and about a month later an answer to the problem of the canoe turned up. "How about us renting a little place here so we can come back for holidays?" Charlie suggested as we were finishing our evening meal.

"Oh come on Charlie, that's a daft idea." Smiling, I lifted Charlotte out of her high chair. "We can't do that, and anyway we've got the cottage for holidays", and I left him having scotched that idea – or so I thought. The next day he came home and placed a large, old metal key on the kitchen table. "There's a very small house in Vittoriosa standing empty. It overlooks Grand Harbour, it's got water and electricity and we can rent it for twenty five pounds a year - if we want it" he said with a grin. "The foreman on the site owns it, and he has a relative, a lady called Rosa, who will keep an eye on it when we are in the UK. Let's at least go and see it."

The Three Cities, Vittoriosa (originally called Birgu), Senglea and Kospicua are surrounded by fortifications built by the Knights at the end of the seventeenth century. Before our visit Charlie borrowed a book from the Maltese foreman and I learnt that, amongst others, the Phoenicians, the Greeks, the Romans, the Byzantines, the Moslem Arabs, the Normans, the Knights of the Order of Hospitallers, the Spanish and, finally, the French had, over the centuries, sailed into Grand Harbour and claimed the islands for themselves until, in 1800, Lord

Nelson's fleet appeared on the horizon. Eventually, after much squabbling, the various powers reached an agreement in 1814 whereby Malta and Gozo became a British colony. Meanwhile, over the centuries, the islanders had become successful pirates, cultivated olive trees and vines, grew cotton for their clothes and head gear and, from the dandelion, borage, thistle and other wild flowers which grew all over the Island every Spring, harvested the delicious honey.

When the Knights arrived in 1530 they chose Birgu as their capital and built a bastioned fort, Fort St. Angelo, on the tip of a promontory on the south side of Grand Harbour. In 1565 the Turks attacked Malta, pounding Birgu from Mount Sciberras on the other side of the harbour. Besieged, defeat faced the Knights, but when the final battle took place in Birgu la Valette and his defenders repulsed their enemy, the siege was lifted, and the Knights honoured Birgu with the name 'Vittoriosa'.

During the Second World War Malta was again besieged this time by the Axis forces. Their strategy was to bomb or starve the Island into submission, achieve an amphibious landing, and then use Malta as a staging post to supply their forces in North Africa. The population was starving and families lived in caves to shelter from the bombing, whilst the areas near Valetta and the medieval Three Cities overlooking Grand Harbour were the main focus of the aerial attacks. British convoys struggled to supply the Island with food, medical supplies and ammunition, and on January 10th 1941 'HMS Illustrious', supporting convoys in the Mediterranean, was attacked. She limped into Grand Harbour, whilst the Germans continued their assault, and The Three Cities were severely damaged, in some places reduced to rubble. Another poignant story told how in March 1941 crowds gathered in the Three Cities to watch three ships, laden with supplies, enter Grand Harbour. Out of a clear blue sky came the bombers, dropped their loads, scored three direct hits, and the ships disappeared under the water. The more I read of Malta's history the reasons for our friend Fred's determination to become a free citizen in his own country became clear.

My newly found knowledge did little to change my opinion that this was one of Charlie's maddest ideas. We drove in to Vittoriosa through the Couvre Porte, one of the three gateways in the fortifications, and headed downhill through the city square towards the waterfront, past centuries old buildings, many still war damaged, others standing despite their walls crumbling onto the dusty roads. After turning into several narrow winding streets leading into a labyrinth of dark alleyways we suddenly emerged from between high, windowless walls on either side into a wide lane hewn out of the rock. On the opposite side ran a low wall, and we realised we were overlooking Kalkara Creek, whilst a jumble of shabby, creamy white buildings of varying heights went to left and right. Metal balconies protruded out of the limestone block walls at different levels laden with clothes, whilst irregularly spaced doors all painted a faded green or brown, disappeared round a corner. There was no shade anywhere, and with heat bouncing off the walls I was very relieved we had left the children with Doris.

As we got out of the car Charlie said "We're looking for number 45 – apparently there's a small metal plate screwed to the wall."

"Number 45 what?"

"Oh, I don't know. He just said the house is in a street that overlooks the water!"

We set off in opposite directions. Immediately covered in dust, perspiration running down my face I cursed myself for being so gullible. The lane sloped gently downwards and then split into two, the part nearest to the low wall on the sea side continuing downhill, whilst the other part next to the buildings provided three shallow steps down to a flat area in front of a green door. I stopped and shouted "This must be it. There's the number on the wall at the side of this door!"

At the thought of escaping from the heat, if only for a minute or two, I happily stood back as Charlie opened the door and we stepped down into a large space, totally empty and very dark apart from a glimmer of light through vents in the shutters covering a small window at the back. In one corner a door led into a room which had a stone sink, a toilet and a cold tap, and in the other corner a metal spiral staircase led up into two rooms. High windows in the big front room opened onto a rusty balcony overlooking Grand Harbour, whilst a windowless room at the back was dark and cool, and large enough for a single bed for Nic and a cot for Charlotte.

From the balcony we could see over the low wall down onto a large outcrop of rock on the edge of the water, where a crowd of young men and boys had gathered, and we watched as they jumped, or flung themselves, into the harbour, obviously the local swimming pool.

"What a fantastic situation!" exclaimed Charlie, and I had to agree. The view from the balcony was spectacular, over the expanse of brilliant blue water of the Creek, out beyond Rinella Bay and beyond again to Fort Ricasoli which, with Fort St.Angelo, had been the two original guardians of the entrance into Grand Harbour.

"It looks awfully deep" I said uncertainly, because I was a very poor swimmer. "I don't think I would swim there – would you?"

"Yes probably, but it must be deep because very big naval ships moor in the Creek regularly. I know it's no good for the canoe, but there must be somewhere round here where I can store it."

I was far from convinced. "I can't see the point. We really don't need a weekend place, and that's all it could be" I protested.

"Yes, but we could come for holidays, it's so cheap and there's no crime here, so I can't see why not. We can just see it as a stone tent!" I knew I had lost the argument.

No-one had lived in the tiny house for about two years, the last occupant having been an elderly relative of the owner, and over the following two weekends we set about cleaning and decorating. After a quick coat of white paint the upstairs rooms were useable, and in a junk shop in Sliema I found an old metal bed, with ornamental brass knobs for us, a small bed for Nic and a cot for Charlotte which, with a small chest and a couple of chairs, was all we needed. Downstairs required more effort. The toilet was filthy but, thankfully, operational with enough room alongside for Charlie to fix a plasterboard partition to provide some privacy. A small two ring electric cooker, a folding table with two more chairs, a large, stout box to hold a couple of pans, cutlery and non-breakable crockery, left just enough space for Charlie to fix two shelves along the back wall, whilst more white paint applied liberally to walls, ceilings and paintwork completed a transformation.

A fortnight later, painting finished, the children safe at home with Doris, we sat on our balcony as darkness approached. The grigalata blew into the upstairs room from the north-east, unexpectedly cool and refreshing after the sticky, humid atmosphere inland. The surface of the darkening, deep, blue water rippled slightly in the breeze, and across Kalkara Creek, on the promontory known as Gallows Point, the battered remains of Fort Ricasoli stood silhouetted against the evening light, the open sea beyond gradually merging into the night sky. Several destroyers and frigates were anchored in the middle of the creek, signal lights winking from their mastheads, the deepest water reserved for them, whilst patrol boats and the local djhaisas steered carefully round the larger vessels.

Around the corner from the little house bells rang out from the parish church dedicated to Saint Lawrence, the patron saint of the poor (and of cooks) and known as the Church of San Lorenzo a Mare. Built in 1681 it was bombed three times during the War, but (our little book informed us) had soon been rebuilt in the baroque style complete with niches, statues and pilasters whilst still surrounded by war damaged dwellings.

Several women hastened past on their way to evening mass, veils over their heads and shoulders, many pausing long enough to look up and smile a welcome to us. Over to our left the lights from Valetta suddenly sprang into life, twinkling brightly along the length of Mount Sciberras down to Fort St. Elmo at the end of the promontory, whilst a small cluster of lights pinpointed the Upper Baracca Gardens below the city. The bells fell quiet. The rocky foreshore had been abandoned by the swimmers. The churchgoers were yet to complete their devotions and return. All was silent, still and magical.

"Shall we go away for the weekend?" Charlie asked the following Thursday with a wry grin.

"Great idea. I'll go and pack!" I replied with a hint of sarcasm – our weekend retreat was all of five miles away!

We took Nic and Charlotte with us, and soon lads of various ages and sizes were knocking on the door asking for Nic to go out to play, but the close proximity of the harbour resulted in a firm "no" from me. He had to be content with playing on the balcony, but the small fishing village of Marsaskala was nearby, and with a sandy beach for the children and a small bar for Charlie, our little getaway suited us all very well.

The stone tent.

GOING HOME

Our final winter and spring in 1965/1966 were pleasant and uneventful. The numbers of Service personnel gradually dwindled, resulting in many farewell parties. Nic was nearly five, in school and learning to read, Charlotte happy in a small nursery, although never free of coughs and colds. I was cast in another play, and Charlie was very busy as the scheme was, at last, making progress with final completion anticipated in a few months. The new power station was officially commissioned in March 1966 and two improvements followed - traffic lights were installed on main roads, and a local TV station opened, replacing the programmes previously provided by Italian television.

Liverpool still seemed very far away - until the end of May. "Look's as if we'll be leaving almost three years to the day we arrived" Charlie announced one evening.

"Really? Right, I'm taking Charlotte upstairs" I replied, not really listening. When I returned he looked up from studying a catalogue which had a very colourful front picture of a cruise ship. With a big grin he asked "Fancy a cruise home? We can have the cost of our flights from the firm and use the money to go back by ship. You hate flying and it'll give us a fixed date we can work to. If we are flying, and then there's a sudden problem here, I'd be expected to postpone our leaving date."

"Great idea! Yes let's decide to do that!" I exclaimed, and

it was settled. We would leave on the 15th August 1966 on the *Achille Lauro*, an Italian ship, joining it for the last week of its six week voyage from Australia to the UK, with a day-long stop in Naples giving us enough time to visit Pompeii as tourists.

For our belongings to be shipped back to the UK we had to pack well ahead of our departure, and decided to vacate the villa at the end of June and spend the last six weeks in our little house. At the site the final weeks revealed unexpected snags and, with an absolute deadline, Charlie was hardly ever at home - so the packing was left to me. In my letters home the true state of the house in Liverpool had been gradually revealed to my parents and, knowing we could not move in to our new home immediately on our return, my mother had written "Come to us for a while. The high chair and cot, and the pram, are still here after Nic" - so ours found new homes in the village. However, during three years we had acquired many things we did not want to leave behind, as well as small items of baby equipment, toys and clothes that Charlotte's arrival had necessitated. Some items we would need as soon as we got back to the UK, whilst others we could manage without until they arrived by sea. Piles of 'needed', 'not needed' and 'Vittoriosa' cluttered the lounge until the packing crates arrived, decisions were made, and it was too late to change my mind.

Peggy and David had already left the Island, and other friends would soon be posted to various far flung parts of the world. We had our last party before leaving the villa during which I watched as friends, old and new, milled around the lounge, in and out of the garden, chatting and laughing, always at ease - as they had to be, because for them everything was temporary, transient, for the moment. After they had left and the villa was quiet, Charlie turned off all the lights in the house and we sat in the garden, the silence broken only by the busy clicking and buzzing of the cicadas, and the gentle swish of water trickling from the mouth of the stone lady in the middle of the pond.

I gazed at the myriad of stars twinkling in the blue-black sky, suddenly unsure of what lay ahead, and to disguise my anxiety said "I'm glad we're leaving - are you?"

"I am" he replied, "and I'm even more glad that we're not going somewhere en-route to somewhere else, as they all are!"

Our last day in the villa arrived. Everything we needed for six weeks in Vittoriosa, and then on the voyage home, was accommodated in four large suitcases standing in the hallway. "I'm leaving now" shouted Charlie as he tied a final knot to the rope attaching the trailer holding the canoe to the bumper of my Morris Minor, and taking the two largest suitcases he set off with Nic.

A tearful Doris held Charlotte in her arms for the last time as I had a final walk in the garden. When the agent arrived to collect the keys Doris handed Charlotte to me with a big, heaving sob, and after a final hug we struggled down the steps with the two remaining suitcases as an ancient Austin taxi came chugging round the corner in the usual cloud of dust. Coming to a halt as he saw us standing on the pavement the rather large driver heaved himself out of the car, pointed at the two cases, and threw his hands in the air.

"Madam, madam that is a difficulty, she will not open!" he exclaimed, pointing at the boot lid, shaking his head. Doris, as ever, came to the rescue and, after a few quiet words in Maltese, room for our luggage on the front seat had been organised. I surrendered the keys to the agent, and Charlotte and I waved "goodbye" to our lovely old villa and to our faithful Doris.

The children settled in the little house as if they had never lived anywhere else. Charlie had not yet sold his scooter, and as I had the car Nic could still go to school and Charlotte to her nursery. Although there appeared to be no other British people living in Vittoriosa our kindly neighbours decided we were acceptable, and soon the local children became frequent visitors with offers of help or just to play. The local baker's oven had been hewn out of the rock round the corner, and one young boy often knocked and said "Madam I am Angelo. The little girl can come with me for the bread?" I knew his mother who lived nearby and, hand and hand, they would go, Charlotte aged two, blonde curls to her shoulders in a bright blue frock, and Angelo aged six, barefoot, black curls encircling his serious young face, returning with several loaves of fresh bread straight out of the oven. Equally, I had no concerns over two young girls who lived a few doors away and would knock politely and ask "the baby girl can come for a walk Madam please?", put Charlotte in her push chair, carefully strap her in, and take her for a walk.

In Vittoriosa there was one big difference – this was not sleepy Birkirkara where I never worried about Nic's safety. When we returned each afternoon I made sure I locked the door in case one of the boys came round and whisked him off, down to the rocks at the edge of the deep harbour water. One afternoon at the beginning of August I returned from collecting Nic from school. He ran up the stairs as I lifted Charlotte from her pushchair and walked up the spiral staircase with her, one step at a time. Before we reached the balcony Nic had opened the french window and was jumping up and down, beside himself with excitement. "Quick, come and look!" he yelled. An enormous American aircraft carrier was moored directly opposite our little house, the Stars and Stripes level with our balcony fluttering in the breeze. With shiny aircraft lined up on its flight deck it was huge and overpowering, the usual naval shipping reduced to insignificance, whilst the djhaisas looked like toys.

I grabbed at Nic as he tried to climb over the balcony, gabbling to the crowd of boys who suddenly appeared, gesticulating to him to go down and join them by their swimming pool. "No you can't go with them. When Charlie comes home he'll take you" I said firmly, and later that evening we joined our neighbours down on the rocks as we all gawped and gasped at the carrier, chattering in a mixture of English and Maltese, totally in awe of this all-powerful American monster. It was so close we could clearly see the sailors in their brilliant white bell bottom trousers and flat caps, and the rows of guns poking out of the side of the vessel. Then, as darkness descended, everyone climbed up the steep limestone steps hewn out of the rock calling "bye bye" and "sahha", and disappeared into the alleyways leading to the Square.

At last the children fell asleep and Charlie and I sat on our balcony with a glass of wine watching the enormous craft lit up and dressed overall, the humming of its generators drifting over the deep water the only sound, a spectacle to rival even San Lorenzo del Mare Church in its festa finery. Next day was Sunday and, up later than usual, I realised there was no noise coming from the little bedroom and looked in. Charlotte was sitting up in her cot, but Nic's bed was empty. "Charlie, Nic's gone!" I yelled my heart in my mouth.

Pulling his shorts on, Charlie dashed downstairs, found the door open, ran across the lane, peered over the low wall at the group of lads on the rocks below, and yelled "Nic where are you?" He recognised one of the bigger boys who smiling broadly, emerged from the crowd holding Nic with one hand, gesticulating to Charlie to join them with the other.

"Joseph, what is Nic doing there? He should be in the house!" Charlie shouted from the bottom of the steps trying not to sound as angry as he felt.

"But Mr. Corke he came to swim with us. He comes many times" Joseph protested as Nic, his pyjama short-bottoms dripping, pulled at his hand saying "Joseph, again, again to the big ship, now, now!"

"The big ship? What's been going on?"

Realising that Charlie was actually angry rather than pleased, Joseph pushed Nic towards his father and said "He came down by himself and we were swimming to the ship and he jumped in with us, and we looked after him, as you can see."

The crowd fell silent and Charlie's anger dissipated as he listened to the boy's explanation. "Thank you Joseph. Yes, you did look after him, and I know he is a good swimmer, but he's only five years old and it is a long way to swim all the way to the middle of the Harbour! Now I will take him to the house, but thank you again."

Whilst they were gone I discovered how Nic had got out - and it was our fault. A second, and then a third, glass of wine had kept us on the balcony. The neighbourhood had fallen silent, the only sounds coming from the ship, low whirring noises from unseen engines or the occasional voice floating over the dark water. Each of us had assumed the other would lock the door, but I found the old metal key sitting on the table, and for the last fortnight I slept with the key under my pillow!

In Vittoriosa the festa dedicated to St. Lawrence was celebrated on the 10th August each year followed by the festa to honour St. Dominic on the last Sunday at the end of the month. Preparations had begun before we arrived. Flags, banners and religious statues attached to pillars lined every street along which the various processions would pass, whilst hand-painted textile pavaljuni, with their elaborate baroque patterns, hung over the route, fluttering in the hot dry wind. St. Lawrence's Church was swathed in garlands of multi coloured electric lights, and as soon as dusk fell and the lights were switched on, tiny waves in the creek, pink, green and white, twinkled until all fell dark again at ten o'clock.

Busy with final preparations I had failed to register that on the day we were leaving, the 15th August 1966, the final of the World Cup between England and Germany was being played. Bunting in red white and blue was draped from balcony to balcony, whilst the Union Jack fluttered on buses, cars and mopeds, and even on bikes being ridden by the local boys – Germany was still the enemy!

We would be sailing at 11pm local time. I took the children to the site office on our last afternoon to bid farewell to everyone, and returned to the little house for a quick meal hoping, in vain, that the children would have a nap before we left. Rosa, employed to guard our house, arrived and inspected each room, talking incessantly. Joseph then arrived with several of the boys, whilst Angelo and the little girls from round the corner completed the gathering. They all crowded round the children, holding their hands, kissing them and stroking Charlotte's hair until I despaired. "Charlie, please help! We're not going to get away in time."

He picked up our one travelling suitcase, the other three having been already deposited at the shipping office, and announced loudly "we are leaving! You will miss the football! Goodbye, good bye!"

"Sahha, sahha, goodbye, goodbye" they all shouted, and disappeared. Five minutes later Rosa returned and Charlie gave her the key as we took a final, hurried look at the little house. Sorry to be leaving these kindly, hospitable people I, rather unsteadily, said "Shall we leave the hood down for our final drive under the Mediterranean sky?"

Regardless of the darkness front doors were open, neighbours sitting outside on the usual hard chairs. Stalls, selling nougat and lemonade for the children and Cisk beer for the men, had been set up randomly amongst the battered, shabby buildings, and everyone was cheering for England. I was close to tears as we set off in my old Morris Minor for the last time. Suddenly a huge roar filled Vittoriosa! News of England's victory had come across the radio. "Hurrah" "hurrah" "hurrah" echoed around the village. Car drivers hooted again and again, boys on scooters raced up and down the roads and narrow alleyways shouting "England for victory!" and, as Charlie slowly made our way through the crowds towards the square women and children hung out of their windows, waving from their balconies calling "Goodbye, goodbye", showering us and the car with multi coloured paper flowers.

SAILING BY

Leaving my car behind, my faithful friend for eight years, was a terrible wrench. Rust had taken its toll on the undercarriage, the tyres were almost bald with their daily pounding on the rough, stony roads, the hood no longer kept out the rain, and to re-import it to the UK would have cost far more than the car was worth.

With little thought of the consequences for the environment, the dumping of vehicles in the sea was, I was told, the standard method of getting rid of old vehicles, and the reason why the Maltese countryside was litter free. I therefore consoled myself with the knowledge that, lying at the bottom of the sparkling blue sea, it would provide homes for the sea creatures that attach themselves to shipwrecks.

The *Achille Lauro* was chained up to three massive stone bollards in a dock on the Valetta waterfront. Before embarking I handed the car keys to the Customs Official who, I was assured, would arrange for its legal disposal at sea in international waters, outside the usual three mile limit. Then, making our way through a huge crowd of excitable people, shouting, whistling and waving their arms, we took the children and ourselves up the gangplank and on to the ship. If we had known that it had suffered a collision in 1953, and an explosion and fire on board only the year before, we might not have been so happy about our keenly anticipated cruise home. An ill-fated ship, the *Achille Lauro* would be the scene of a high-jacking and murder of a passenger in 1985, and eventually sink in the Indian Ocean near Somalia after another explosion in the engine room.

It carried about a thousand passengers and crew, and excited family members were hugging and kissing their loved ones as they disembarked, whilst other groups of tearful parents were shepherded off the ship in readiness for our departure, leaving behind smartly dressed young men, presumably emigrating to the UK to find work, smoking nervously as they waited to wave a final goodbye.

The trip started badly. Bedding on the bunks in our four berth cabin had not been changed, the tiny bathroom was filthy and a strange smell hung in the air despite the open porthole. Charlie found a steward who threw his arms in the air and let forth a stream of abuse in Italian when asked to sort out our cabin. "I hope they're not all like him!" Charlie exclaimed. "Let's go up on deck whilst he cleans the cabin, the air's so warm the kids will be fine."

We found a space amongst the crowds hanging over the railings of the ship overlooking the quayside, and watched the comings and goings of the crew members, and countless officials in smart uniforms, carrying sheaves of papers, jostling with one another, but with no obvious destination. Midnight came and went and, at last, the engines revved up, and smoke poured out of the ship's two funnels into the dark sky. The enormous chains were removed from the stone bollards and slowly we started to move, djhaisas scurrying out of the way as white topped slews of black, oily, churned-up water rushed towards the harbour walls.

As we pulled away from the massive fortifications built by the Knights so long ago the bright lights of Valetta, twinkling along the length of Mount Sciberras to the tip of the promontory, came into view. We headed towards the open sea, past the end of Dockyard Creek, then Kalkara Creek, lights from the Three Cities flickering in the black water. Gradually gathering speed we left Fort St. Angelo behind as we approached Fort Ricasoli on Gallows Point on one side and Fort St. Elmo on the seaward shore of Mount Sciberras on the other. Lights signalling the position of the breakwater shone brightly ahead, and we were out at sea. The romance of leaving our Mediterranean home under a starlit sky kept us on board until the lights of Malta were no more than tiny pin pricks shimmering faintly on the horizon. I stared into the warm darkness, my mind turning to our unknown future with some trepidation, but also excitement until Charlie, always the realist, exclaimed "Well, that's that! Come on, let's get the kids to bed," and taking one child each we made our way down through the ship.

In our freshly cleaned cabin we settled down to enjoy our mini holiday. Nic spent most of his time at the swimming pool with several boys of a similar age, and Charlotte enjoyed playing with other small children, but the gap in the railings was far from child proof and I spent my time making sure she stayed away from them. We sailed into the Bay of Naples on a calm sea in brilliant sunshine, Vesuvius in the distance, gently puffing small clouds of steam into the brilliant blue sky. After disembarking we made our way to Pompeii, on the way buying freshly picked bananas from a street vendor, so delicious that the flavour remains with me to this day. We wandered through the remains of the ancient city where life for its citizens had been frozen in time when it was buried under tons of ash and pumice after Vesuvius erupted in AD79. A snapshot of Roman life and evidence of the wealth and luxury which had been enjoyed by its citizens was still obvious inside the ruins of the houses and public buildings.

The ship however was far from luxurious, bearing all the signs of heavy use during the five weeks it had been at sea. Most of the toys in the nursery were broken, as were the irons in the laundry, and the taps on the wash basin. The seats on many dining room chairs were ripped, whilst the sofas in the lounges were missing a caster, sometimes two. Food was endless spaghetti, and even the wine was rough.

At least the weather was kind to us until we entered the Bay of Biscay on the sixth day and ran into a summer storm. Bucking and heaving we steamed on, the sky grey and heavy with rain, clouds racing in a wind that buffeted our ears as we made our way along the decks. Charlie, who had always claimed to be seasick when crossing the Mersey on the ferry as a child, had found his sea legs and, despite the weather, we all ventured to the restaurant which was almost empty as we faced our final meal of spaghetti and veal.

Back in our cabin the children were asleep, the suitcase packed for a quick getaway the following morning, "Come on deck" Charlie suggested. "I've been, and it's really wonderful! The moonlight is making the waves effervescent, and there are dolphins trailing the ship and you can see them leaping out of the water!"

It sounded very romantic and I ventured up the stairs towards the deck. Moonlight glistened on the slippery deck, the wind howled around my head, a strong gust hurtled down the steps and the ship rolled as a huge wave sent water sloshing over the railings. Suddenly I was terrified, and grabbing the handrail on the stairway I shouted into the wind "sorry, it's too scary!" and bolted back to the lounge – we were returning to a British summer.

By the morning the sea was calm once more and soon we were in sight of the south coast, and as we disembarked in Portsmouth I vowed I would never go on a cruise ship again. Waiting to collect our hire car Charlie said "Could you ring your Mum and ask her if we can have steak and onions tonight? I never want to see spaghetti again!"

We drove to North Wales where delighted grandparents welcomed us home. The children and I settled in at my parents' house, while Charlie gave himself a week's holiday in his beloved cottage with his parents. He and his father tackled work which

Grandpa had not been able to carry out on his own, whilst his mother fed him his favourite puddings and fruit cake and generally made a fuss of him.

One evening, leaving the children with my parents and borrowing my mother's car, I went to the cottage. Leaving the car at the bottom of the lane I made my way up slowly, breathing in the cool air, sniffing happily at the mounds of dark pink heather, revelling in the restful dark green colour of the pine trees disappearing into the distance. From the top of the bank I saw Charlie and his parents sitting on the wall opposite the old plum trees, and as I walked down the grass steps Grandpa had cut into the bank I heard Charlie ask " What's the outside rendering on the house like?"

There was a pause "Well, if you really want to know, it's bad" I heard his father say. "It's cracked and peeling and you can tell it's not been touched since before the last War. The windows haven't a lick of paint on the frames, neither has the front door. I had a look up the side where the subsidence is obvious, and the back garden's a jungle."

"I'd better warn Jan then."

"Would be as well" replied his father and, as he looked up and saw me, added "because if the inside is as bad as the outside you're both in for a bit of a shock!"

AFTERWORD

The old Victorian house was rather more than a bit of a shock, and plans for holidays in Malta went on hold. For several years, with help from his long suffering father, we laboured to make the house habitable, whilst Charlie set up his own civil engineering consultancy and I worked for a large legal firm in Liverpool. The arrival in 1969 of another lovely daughter, Emma, made our holiday plans even less likely until early in 1971, and for no obvious reason, the inevitable happened – Charlie remembered his canoe.

"I think it's time we had a proper holiday" he announced. "Why don't we drive to Malta, and then we can bring the canoe back on top of the car?"

During the five years that had passed since our return home two groups of friends had stayed in the little house. Rosa's habit of engaging them in conversation about England, and her burning desire to have a holiday in the UK, had been somewhat problematic, but they reported that the canoe was still stored round the corner in an old cave.

Emma was not quite two and I had not yet returned to work, but Charlie had had a busy year in his practice, and our finances were reasonably secure. Laughing, I said "It's an awfully long way to go for a canoe – why don't you buy one if you really want to go canoeing?"

His face was a picture. "Jan, I filled all those evenings

when I was in Malta on my own making it! You weren't there in that barn of a place, echoing like a church every time I made a noise! I put a lot of work into that canoe, and now its thousands of miles away and I can't use it!"

I could see I would have to find very good reasons why we should not drive to Malta and decided to look at the map. The quickest route was to go through the (then) new Mont Blanc Tunnel, but we would still have to drive two and a half thousand miles. Also there were three ferries - Dover to Calais, then the Straits of Messina from main land Italy to Sicily and finally overnight from Syraceuse to Malta.

I folded the map carefully as I marshalled my arguments. "How long d'you reckon it'll take to drive?" I asked.

"A week each way and four weeks on the Island. If we go early in June there'll be six available weeks before starting on the next job" he replied. "Italy has miles of motorways, so we could stop each night and camp on the way."

I swallowed before exclaiming "Charlie, that's a bit much! I know you can set up camp quickly, but you'll have to do it every evening. With the three children we'll have to take loads of camping gear, as well as the pushchair for Emma. It's just not feasible!"

Realising he was up against a reasonable argument he changed tack. "Yes, fair enough, but if we had a bigger car the kids can sleep in the car, and then we only need a small two man tent for us. One big suitcase for clothes will be enough because it'll be hot. I'll go and have a look at some cars."

A couple of weeks passed with no further mention of a trip to Malta until he came home and announced he'd solved the problem. "After supper will you come and have a look at a car I've found?" he asked. "If you think it's OK we can have another chat about the holiday." He had found a new to us (second hand) Ford Cortina Estate car. It could accommodate all our camping gear, and had back seats large enough for Nic and Charlotte to sleep on - "with slight modifications" he promised.

"But Emma needs somewhere to sleep!"

"Oh I've thought about that. I can fit out the boot as a safe cot for her and she can sleep all the way there."

"Yes" I replied, "but Charlotte is too big for the cot in the little house. We'd have to get another small bed, and put Emma in the old cot – I suppose we can squeeze another bed into the room." To my surprise I was suddenly quite excited about the holiday.

"That's fine. I'll send money to Rosa and she can get one." All was settled.

At the beginning of June 1971 we were on our way to Malta for six weeks. The end of the first long day found us in France with no mishaps, the children asleep in the car, Charlie eagerly anticipating the experience of driving through the Mont Blanc Tunnel. Opened to traffic in 1965 it was seven and a quarter miles long, three times longer than any existing highway tunnel at that time. Built as a single gallery twenty eight feet wide, with only one lane in each direction, the French/Italian consortium that had built the tunnel had seen it as the obvious choice for long distance haulage between France and Italy, but clearly they had not anticipated the huge growth in Trans/Alpine traffic.

Next day we drove into a yawning, black hole with no street lighting, down to a depth of over eight thousand feet under the summit of the Aiguille de Midi. Long convoys of huge lorries thundered past in the opposite direction, sometimes our respective wing mirrors almost touching. I held my breath, shrank back into my seat, and closed my eyes, cursing that I had ever agreed to the holiday – and we were still in France!

Italian Engineering

Emerging at last into bright sun shine in the Aosta Valley was such a relief we allowed ourselves an unscheduled stop for delicious Italian ice creams before setting off on the autostrada. Day after day we drove, mile after mile of motorway, plunging into long, dark tunnels or crossing over deep valleys where concrete pillars supporting the road disappeared into the rocky landscape, two or three hundred feet below. We skirted round Milan, Genoa, and Pisa, and bypassed Rome and Naples, heading to the westernmost tip of southern Italy to catch the ferry across the Straits of Messina to Sicily. Barely more than a channel in the Mediterranean the Straits is less than two miles in width, and in less than an hour we were in Sicily.

For our last night "on the road" we decided to find somewhere to stay in Catania, the final town of any size before

Syraceuse. A building on the outskirts, 'Albergo' flashing above the door, looked promising and we were desperate to sleep in a bed after six nights on the ground in our tiny tent. A very grumpy woman, having taken our money, led us to a huge gloomy room where we found a cot for Emma, one single bed for Nic and Charlotte to share and an old metal double bed with a mattress so thin and hard that I longed for the tent!

"Don't fancy any food here. Let's find a café somewhere" Charlie suggested in the morning. We set off to walk into the town and within a few minutes saw a crowd of large men approaching us, gesticulating and pointing at the children. Suddenly I was very apprehensive. It was the era when kidnapping by the mafia was rampant, and we were the only obvious strangers in a narrow, sunless street.

"Don't like the look of these" I muttered as they continued towards us, filling the confined space. As I tried to manoeuvre the pushchair round them the largest man pointed at Charlotte with her blonde hair and blue eyes, swooped down on her, swung her up in the air, twirled her round, put her down again crying out "bellissima bambina" over and over again, shook our hands, and carried on down the street!

"Stop worrying about the mafia!" Charlie exclaimed. "Stories about them are just exaggerated for the newspapers at home."

The weekly ferry from Syraceuse to Malta was scheduled to leave at six, and after a leisurely drive we arrived at the port late in the afternoon. A treeless area alongside the water appeared to be the car park, with concrete bollards at regular intervals to ensure cars did not fall into the Mediterranean. A few cars were already parked, and Charlie reversed carefully into a space, the bumper touching one of the bollards.

With a couple of hours to spare we decided to have a nap and were settling into our seats when there was a sharp rap on the driver's side window. Two very officious men in uniform with guns in their holsters were glaring into the car, at the same time opening the doors and shouting "aperto, aperto!" As Charlie got out they grabbed the keys from the ignition and, with one on either side, marched him into a small building nearby, with 'POLIZIA' on a sign above the door.

Emma started to howl, Charlotte to cry and for once Nic was silent. I felt utterly helpless and could do nothing but try to comfort and reassure them as we waited, and waited, our eyes fixed on the door of the little building. An hour passed as more cars arrived, and I decided I would approach a family who had smiled at us when they saw Emma in her pushchair, with Charlotte clutching the handles. Italian phrase book in hand I took a deep breath and said to the children "I am going to ask those nice people if they can help us."

As I walked over to their car Nic suddenly shouted "Dad! Dad! He's coming!" Looking over I saw Charlie emerge from the building, his hand in the back pocket of his very shabby and bedraggled shorts where he always kept his wallet. He walked over, grinned and said "Well, that's that! Apparently I had damaged the bollard!" Were we in mafia country after all?

Six o' clock came and went, as did seven, and then eight with no sign of the ferry. The friendly Italian family spoke faltering English and I had my phrase book, and between us we managed a reasonable conversation. They travelled to Malta regularly and assured me the ferry would arrive, but had no idea when, and I began to wonder if we would ever complete the final sixty miles of our marathon journey. About eight thirty a rather ancient boat came into view, two funnels belching black smoke into the darkening sky, and drew alongside with much shouting and cheering from those awaiting the arrival of friends and relatives.

Charlie drove the car over a very wobbly wooden gangplank, and as I led the children onto the deck an elderly priest came across to help me, again exclaiming "bellissima bambina" as he took Charlotte by the hand.

By about ten thirty we were underway into the night. The air was still, balmy and warm and we sat on deck, Emma asleep on my knee, Charlotte next to me wrapped within the habit of the elderly priest and Nic, wide awake, held firmly in an iron grip by his father.

We chugged steadily through the calm, night sea, no other ships in sight until, waking from an uncertain doze with a start, I stared into the blue-black darkness where, far off, a tiny speck of light flickered and then another and another, all dancing on the tiny waves, until the lights of Malta lined the horizon. We sailed past the breakwater at daybreak, past the ends of Dockyard Creek and Kalkara Creek into Grand Harbour, the walls and fortifications surrounding Valetta towering above us.

Arriving for our holiday

By the time we had disembarked, the familiar heat was building up as we drove round the Marsa, past the site where Charlie had been working, up to the fortifications and through the Couvre Porte into Vittoriosa. Nothing had changed, and Nic recognised the little house as soon as we drove through the narrow alleyway between the high, windowless walls onto the lane. Rosa, standing by the shabby green door, started waving as we drove round the corner, and after she had proudly shown me the bed she had bought, she scurried away. We still had various bits of food in our cool box, enough to make a breakfast of sorts whilst Charlie went to the grocer's shop in the Square, and after a long sleep in proper beds we had all settled in

Our month's holiday was everything we hoped for. The children loved the beaches, and we visited Doris, now married with children of her own. We met up with Fred, and the local boys who took Nic back into their gang where he spent hours jumping on and off the rocks into the Harbour. Another little boy aged about eight took a shine to Charlotte and came round every day to fetch her to visit his family, or to go to the local baker who still cooked bread in the oven hewn out of the rock.

The canoe was exactly where Charlie had left it. Bars had been fitted on the roof of the car to transport it back to the UK so, rounding up the lads, Charlie got it onto the roof and took it back to Marsaskala. Such was Malta in 1971 – he left the canoe on the beach where no-one touched it, and took the children, ours and half the neighbourhood, for trips before it got too hot, or later in the afternoon.

Rosa was rather eccentric and, although married, she had no children, but sadly I soon decided not to trust Emma into her care. "Charlie, I don't think we should leave the key with Rosa this time" I said. We went to her relative's address, but no-one answered the door, and a second visit had the same result - and we returned to the UK, the key remaining with Rosa.

Several Service people we had known, now retired, were still around and invited us to the Club where we all reminisced happily until one of them asked "Janet, what happened to your old car?"

"It was an awful wrench, handing the keys to the chap at Customs before we got on the ship, but Charlie was right, it just wasn't worth taking it back to the UK" I replied. "There was rust on it everywhere and the hood was full of holes, but I read somewhere it'll be like a reef, a sort of habitat for marine life, so I don't feel too unhappy about it."

Everyone went quiet. Our friend, very embarrassed, asked "Who told you that? Don't you know what happens?"

I stared at him. "Yes, it had to be exported off the Island or dumped in the sea outside the three mile limit and because we didn't export it, it was dumped." I looked at Charlie who, like everyone else, was looking at his feet.

"Jan" said our friend, "I thought you might have seen it driving around, that's why I asked you where it was. The cars are never dumped, that's why there are so many old British cars everywhere. The minute you were out of sight that Customs chap would have found the fellow who had already bought it to give him the keys. It's a big racket, everyone knows about it."

I didn't know whether to laugh or cry. "I need a stiff drink!" I said a bit unsteadily, as Charlie came over and said "I'm really sorry Jan, but I knew you'd never have agreed to leave it behind if I told you what would happen!" I knew he was right but didn't forgive him for a long time!

Each day the thermometer crept up and it was time to go home. The boys helped Charlie bring the canoe back from the beach and rope it securely to the roof of the car, where it provided a perfect nesting place for a very large, and very smelly, turtle shell that Nic had found on the beach and insisted should return with us.

Unlike our original leave-taking we were starting early in the morning. I decided not to tell Rosa exactly when we were leaving until the night before, but in the morning she wept over the girls, hugged Nic and clutched my arm until Charlie handed her the key and got in to the car. The boys chased us all the way up the alleyways into the Square, waving and shouting "bye bye "until we were out of sight.

"Can't we stay longer?" exclaimed Nic.

"I know. It's been great, but cheer up, we can come again soon" I replied.

Back on the big ferry to Syraceuse, then the little ferry over the Straits of Messina and then the long drive through southern Italy, now dry and completely parched where nothing grew. Tall concrete chimneys spewed out evil-looking yellow smoke into the cloudless sky and the air throbbed with heat as we skirted Cosenza. Bowling along at a steady eighty miles per hour we were approaching the outskirts of Rome but slowed slightly as a jumble of stationary cars and blue flashing lights on the other side of the motorway signalled a crash. The autostrada was almost empty and a few minutes later we stopped on the wide shoulder under a road bridge, desperate to find shelter whilst we ate bread, cheese and tomatoes, our staple diet when driving, and drank tepid water from our plastic container. Suddenly a large black car appeared in the distance on our side of the autostrada and seconds later hurtled past us, followed by an enormous hearse with two coffins inside rocking from side to side, both vehicles going at about a hundred miles an hour.

"Dad, look at that speed!" Nic exclaimed, jumping about with excitement. "Where are they going?"

"Ambulance chasing" Charlie replied. I was relieved Nic didn't understand what he meant.

The following day we left the campsite early enough to drive into the centre of Rome. "I came here about twenty five years ago on my motor bike. It's all changed so much I don't think we better stop " said Charlie, "but I know how to get back to the motorway." Two hours later, in the midday heat, we were driving around the enormous white marble Victor Emmanuel II Monument for the fifth time, Emma howling miserably, Charlotte trying not to cry, and Nic thumping the back of the passenger seat with his feet. I exploded.

"Charlie, if you do not stop the next person we see, and ask the way back to the autostrada I'm opening my door at the next traffic lights and getting out! Do you hear me?"

He did stop and I did not get out at the next traffic lights, and within half an hour we were back on the motorway heading north.

One trip through the Mont Blanc Tunnel was enough and we decided to go back over the Alps. We headed for Milan arriving there in the evening, resigned to spending a night in the car. The city was a maelstrom of cars, lorries, buses and scooters and, despite the fumes, Charlie was driving with his window open trying to catch some cool air as we made our way through the city. The children, mesmerised by the neon lights, bustle of people and noisy traffic, were wide awake as we stopped at a large junction, where three sets of traffic lights had to be negotiated, as well as mad drivers hooting loudly and ducking and diving between lorries and buses.

Suddenly a youngish woman, with blonde curly hair, black eyes heavily made-up, barred red lips showing brown discoloured teeth and a spectacular cleavage appeared from nowhere. Sticking one arm through the open window and grabbing the handle on Charlie's door with the other, she tried to wrench it open.

"Caro, you are lost si? I come with you!" she cried.

We were so startled that for a moment there was silence then I yelled "get out, get out!" just as the lights turned green.

Pandemonium erupted. Cars behind hooted at us repeatedly, and within seconds we were the centre of a traffic jam, scooters, cars and huge lorries trying to avoid us as the lady of the night disappeared, leaving us to thread our way through the chaos as a little voice from the back asked "What did that nice lady want Mummy?"

With no more mishaps, four days later we arrived in. Liverpool. "Back to normal, that'll be nice" I said as we unloaded the car, but it was not to be. Earlier in the year the Post Office workers had gone on strike again, Rolls Royce had gone into administration, unemployment had been rising inexorably throughout the year, and the 'troubles' in Northern Ireland were going from bad to worse. Unsurprisingly, fears about the economy had worsened whilst we were away, a big housing scheme Charlie had been engaged to work on had been cancelled - and I had no job.

Back to normal – but not quite.

Charlie's itchy feet sent him looking for another ruin that needed rescuing. He discovered a Victorian mansion overlooking Sefton Park that had been converted into an Army hospital and then abandoned after the Second World War. Negotiations with Liverpool City Council, setting up a building company, and converting the property into nineteen flats was a huge undertaking which he completed by 1974, despite miners strikes, the working week limited to three days to save electricity, and financial chaos throughout the mid-seventies.

The years went by as we negotiated our way through life with its complications and unforeseen events. Meanwhile we told brave friends that the little house was available and some went on visits, always reporting that Rosa had become very strange, turning up at the crack of dawn with gifts of food, or late at night with religious statues. After about ten years we relinquished the key to Rosa and our dream of regular holidays in the sun, but throughout we kept the canoe which came with us many years later on another big adventure, a bookshop near the sea in South Devon.

Old Vittoriosa